Affairs

Mary Anne Wollison

THE SECRET
LIVES OF
WOMEN

Musson/*Toronto*
A member of the General Publishing Group

First published in 1982 by Musson,
a division of General Publishing Co. Limited,
30 Lesmill Road,
Don Mills, Ontario,
M3B 2T6

Canadian Cataloguing in Publication Data

Wollison, Mary Anne.
   Affairs: the secret lives of women

ISBN 0-7737-0063-3

1. Adultery – Canada – Case studies.
2. Women – Psychology.   3. Women –
Canada – Sexual behavior.
I. Title.

HQ806.W65   306.7'36   C82-094691-5

ISBN 0-7737-0063-3
Printed and bound in Canada

Contents

Acknowledgment

A special thank-you to the Golden Muse, and especially, Helene Hoffman, for their efforts and encouragement throughout the writing of this book. Particular thanks to Dr. William Fisher, Dr. Norman Thomas, all the friends and especially the wonderful women whose time and co-operation made this book a reality.

M.A.W.

Introduction

You are about to be introduced to more than twenty women, many of whom are still deeply in love with their mates and all of whom have had at least one affair.

For some of the women whose experiences you will find on these pages, an affair was accompanied by intense upheavals, profound feelings, and a sense of danger arising from the fear of discovery. For others, their experiences were casual diversions that apparently had little or no effect on their marriages. Tina, for example, had no desire to leave her husband, nor could she honestly say that he was not her ideal mate. However, she reveals a complex and contradictory personality: she could no more be content in the arms of one man than she could be content with a single change of clothes. Margo, in contrast, totally misread her husband, and his discovery of her "other life" led to violence, humiliation, and divorce.

The women who were interviewed for this book were frank in their admissions and in their language; their names have been altered, as have the names of the cities where they live. Because their anonymity was guaranteed, these women have bared themselves, revealing the fullness of their secret lives, to offer the reader a portrait of the real women behind the veil of social respectability.

Affairs: The Secret Lives of Women was conceived at a luncheon when the assembled women began discussing various extramarital relationships they had had. Elspeth admitted that, when her husband was out of town, she picked up a man in a bar and slept with him. She feigned guilt, but her animation and the glint in her eyes belied her claims of conscience. Marta, who's slightly overweight, admitted that when her husband ignored her sexually for months on end, she allowed herself to be picked up on a train to Montreal. René revealed that she had a secret lover and that her affair was long-term.

One expects men to boast of affairs and conquests; such behavior is accepted readily and is usually referred to as locker-room talk. Were the women merely boasting? To answer that question, I interviewed women from all walks of life. Most were married, or have been. Some were young; some middle-aged. They were professional women, homemakers, part-time workers. Some had children; others did not. Many were highly educated while others left school early; some were happy in their marriages while others were not. The interviews suggest that the women at the luncheon were not merely bragging; rather, a growing number of women are becoming as bold sexually as are their male counterparts.

Apparently a growing number are also becoming bolder about divulging their affairs. Word of mouth snowballed into contacts, phone calls, letters, and interviews. Whenever I traveled, attended a social event, dropped into a bar, or spoke to a friend, I seemed to meet or hear about yet another woman who had a story to tell.

Many of these women felt they were less dependent on men than their predecessors. The reasons they gave for this feeling varied, but they usually included education, a career, and financial independence. Because these women felt—and were—independent, they wanted equality and felt justified in demanding affection, recognition, and sexual freedom—the same freedom accorded to men.

The new science of sociobiology defines the reasons for independence and the desires that accompany it. Sociobiologists claim that since the dawn of the human species, women have evolved greatly. Unlike other female animals, women can enjoy sex when they are not biologically in heat (ovu-

lati   it of birth control, they need
no   actors, claim sociobiologists,
ha   nique in the animal kingdom.
                               purely out of lust?
                               ws, and the majority selected
fc   this is not true. Instead, our
d   re born of loneliness or a lack
o   n have become more involved
w   , their women have grown iso-
la   eir loneliness has resulted in a
w   ly ended in a search for some
fc
                               l one kind of independence, they
al   That dependency, with rare exception, is _____   eed for reassurance that their animal magnetism exists; the need to touch, to feel, and to be
held, apart from the penetration of the actual sexual act; the
need, as so many put it, "to feel loved." And even when
women know they have the respect of the community or the
respect of their colleagues, they still reveal a need to be respected by their lovers.

Affairs, both casual and serious, are increasing among the
female population, but many women are still isolated and
inhibited; many believe they are the only married woman
within their particular community to have had an affair. This
book is written with those women in mind; it is an effort to
share the experience of the affair with other women who feel
uncomfortable with either their desires or their actions. It is
also written for men, for within the interviews is the answer
to the question, "What do women want?" It is not a one-
word answer: women want attention, respect, mental stimulation, good sexual technique, and what so many describe
as "just caring."

1 Perspectives

Statistics reveal that a substantial number of married men have an affair at some point during their marriages. Western society has, with rare exception, accepted the idea of "male sexual need." The facts beg the question, "Who are these sexually free males having affairs with?" With the exception of the homosexual male, the obvious answer is: with women.

In the past, as recently as 1959, women who involved themselves in sexual liaisons outside marriage were branded as fast, easy, tramps, chippies, whores, sluts, and other unpleasant terms. In fact, women who enjoyed sex within marriage were often condemned with the same degrading verbal abuse. But few of the women interviewed for this book would accept such designations; they demand the right to be free sexually without condemnation.

Today, women's extramarital affairs are being openly discussed by men, by the media, and by women themselves. Reliable statistics on the number of women involved in sex outside marriage are hard to come by, but extrapolations from data assembled by sociological researchers indicate a growing number of women who feel free to express themselves sexually both within and outside of traditional marriage.

Let us examine three reasonably reliable studies: *The Kinsey Report on Female Sexuality* (1953), Morton Hunt's survey (1972), and Tavris and Sadd's *The Redbook Report on Female Sexuality* (1978).

EXTRAMARITAL AFFAIRS

	Women	Men
Kinsey (1953)	26%	50%
Hunt (1972)	25%	50%

REDBOOK
(1978)

This report dealt with women only. It is broken down by age and employment status.

Age	Full-Time Employed	Housewives
25	21%	17%
25–34	40%	23%
35–39	53%	24%
40 +	47%	35%

The mean or average number of women having affairs was given as 29% by *Redbook*. Of these women, 50% had one partner while 90% had fewer than five partners.

Women who had extramarital affairs rated marriage as:

Very Good	Good	Fair	Poor	Very Poor
19%	30%	49%	54%	65%

Women who had extramarital affairs rated sex as:

Very Good	Very Poor
22%	48%

While these data do not suggest a significant overall upsurge in women's extramarital affairs, they do suggest that women who are employed full-time are having more extramarital affairs.

Since 1978, more women have joined the work force, but, more significant, many have taken over managerial positions. There are more highly educated women in the work force today than there have been before, and there is a definite correlation between education and liberalized sexual attitudes.

The percentage of women younger than twenty-five years of age who have engaged in sexual relationships (premarital as opposed to extramarital) has increased threefold in the twenty-nine years since the Kinsey report, according to surveys and studies.

Talking with the Experts

Most psychologists, marriage counsellors, and social workers admit to seeing an increase in the number and frequency of extramarital affairs, particularly among women. The popular notion that women are driven to extramarital relationships is, at best, oversimplified. Dr. William Fisher, from the department of psychology at the University of Western Ontario, feels that women have two main motives in seeking extramarital affairs. The first appears to be dissatisfaction and boredom with their marriage; the second motivation is called "the six-percent solution." Dr. Fisher believes that six percent of all wives who have extramarital relationships have good marriages and fulfilling sex within the marriage, but are seeking the exotic and a kind of sexual renewal. For these women, sex becomes a leisure-time activity. The latter group are more in control of their lives and more aware of what they want. Dr. Fisher's observations seem to be upheld in many of the interviews.

Dr. Norman Thomas, a psychologist and marriage counsellor, has dealt with situations involving extramarital affairs and has found motivations similar to those cited by Dr. Fisher. But Dr. Thomas places a special emphasis on marriage dissatisfaction. He comments on the following questions:

M.A.W.: How common are extramarital affairs?

DR. THOMAS: Affairs are more common among men. What usually brings men in to see me is that their wives are upset. Men also come in when they're edgy or tense. They think if the marriage doesn't shape up, they may stray. They feel guilty beforehand for their thoughts.

Affairs are not usually something people pre-plan. Most people who have affairs feel dissatisfied. They think or feel there's something going on in their personal relationship they don't like. Generally, the problems in a marriage come before the affairs begin.

There are the occasional times when a person goes away to a convention and is having a good time and is not thinking about his wife. An opportunity presents itself and he wonders: why not? Those types of affairs occur frequently with men. When the male leaves home, he leaves home.

Women, especially if they're married with children, tend to take a part of their home life with them wherever they go. Their conscience goes with them. Although women may be out having a great time, their concern about their family is not very far in the background. When the opportunity for a fling presents itself, although they're enjoying themselves and think it might be fun, their conscience takes over. Their concern for their family acts as a kind of barrier and gives them time to check their impulses.

On the other hand, the male, more often than not, is just himself out there, and his wife and kids are way back in the background. After he's done it, he thinks, "Oh, my God, what did I do?"

The majority of men do feel some remorse about having an affair. What they do about the remorse is something else. Lots of them try to admit they don't feel guilty about it. They put on a big bravado act or they try to rationalize or justify it.

M.A.W.: In your experience, what are the reasons for women having extramarital affairs?

DR. THOMAS: Basically it seems to be a lack of communication in marriage. Sometimes there is a dissatisfaction with the sex act itself. Quite often, the person doesn't come to that conclusion immediately. The woman may put it under the guise, "He doesn't care about me," or "I'm just being used." Straight sex—sex on its own—is never the problem. There always seems to be a reduced sense of affection or caring. A woman feels her husband takes her for granted, so she finds someone who makes her feel treasured. If the sex act is an insensitive, inconsiderate experience, she finds someone who makes her feel good. If the sex act is insensitive then the woman begins to feel like a possession, and as if she's being used. I've told fellows you can't follow those how-to-books. You can't just kiss her twice, push something here, and reach for her and find her ready. I've said to men, "Do you think she's a stove? You turn her on and she lights up?"

If that's what's going on, then the woman probably wonders what the point is. There's no real passion, caring, or feeling about the other person. There's a lack of being together on something.

M.A.W.: In your opinion, do affairs affect marriage adversely?

DR. THOMAS: More often than not, they do. I don't think they should. More often than not, an affair will adversely affect a relationship based on a feeling of attachment or being in love rather than a genuine feeling of caring. If I'm attached to you or in love with you, then I project all my attitudes onto you. You are responsible for my sexuality and my happiness. If someone talks to you, they are then threatening my happiness. I'll begin to see you as an extension of myself rather than a person in your own right. In these kinds of situations, there is a tremendous amount of jealousy and possessiveness. In this situation an affair will break the marriage asunder. I don't think it necessarily has to have that effect. The affair can be used as a building block. Because you've had an affair, it doesn't make you a terrible person. The insight you get from an affair should cause some decision-making. People have to decide if they want the marriage or what they found in the affair. They may go back to the marriage and make an attempt at it. They can decide where the marriage went wrong. If they want the relationship, they can work on how they can make it better.

M.A.W.: How does a husband react to knowledge of his wife's affair?

DR. THOMAS: There are different reactions. A woman is generally more tolerant of a husband's affair. One client I'm seeing now was quite hurt when he found out about his wife's affair. He didn't get violently angry and threaten to kick her out. He said he wished she hadn't, but he wondered where he went wrong. He's willing to work on the marriage, but he still gets suspicious when she goes out. That's something they'll have to work on, but he's handling it quite nicely.

Other men will say, "No go, that's it!" One man, whose wife had an affair ten years ago, still finds it a hurting point. It's still something he hasn't forgotten. If a person is reasonably sensitive and can look at his wife as a person, then loving and caring in time will heal that feeling. It's only ego and pride that have been hurt on both sides. The spouse will wonder what people will think of him. They were supposed to have a contract and someone violated it. A husband may see his wife as soiled. That comes from the whole notion of the wife as a chattel or possession. A woman becomes a part of the house.

M.A.W.: Have you dealt with many couples who had agreements about affairs?

DR. THOMAS: I had two, but neither worked out too well. It became a competition. The idea became, "If you're going to do something, then I'm going to do it too." One partner would say, "I had a fantastic time. What about you? My partner is better looking than your partner."

There is something lacking when people have to lock themselves into this arrangement. The affairs almost become the reason for living together. Yet the couple give everything to other people without giving enough to their relationship at home and giving it a chance to blossom.

I think these situations arise because someone feels that, to be a person, he/she must look for something outside the self. For this type of person to feel good about the self, he/she has to find something out there. It's not generated by the marriage if it's not found in the individual. The attitude of the individual is selfish. Their attitude is: "If I want something to make me feel good, and I'm not getting it, it's because you're not giving it to me."

But no one can supply what's missing in someone else. It's like a woman who doesn't have orgasms claiming it's her husband's fault. It's not really her husband's fault. A husband can't give his wife an orgasm; a wife gives them to herself. A woman has to allow herself to get into the sex act sufficiently and an orgasm will occur. If you try to have one, you won't. If you say it's your husband's duty to give you one, then you won't have one for sure. You might look around and find someone who you have an orgasm with because at that moment you allow yourself to let go. You think, "Oh, boy, he's the man for me!" It has nothing to do with him, but everything to do with you. It depends on how much you're prepared to be vulnerable, how much you're prepared to relax, and how much you're prepared to let go.

M.A.W.: How much of a role does sexual chemistry play in attracting people?

DR. THOMAS: There is something to chemistry in terms of the amount of energy you portray. A person who has a lot of energy is going to attract people because people are attracted to sources of energy. If a guy walks into a bar and looks nice and smells nice and walks with a certain determination, then at a very primitive level he instills confidence in a woman. The message such a person sends is: "I'm strong." The message received is: "I feel safe with this person because he is going to protect me."

When people feel safe, then they allow themselves to be vulnerable. If another guy walks in who is every bit as handsome, but he shuffles his feet and hunches his shoulders, then he looks insecure. There is nothing going out—no energy. He is a loser.

There is chemistry, but it depends on the degree to which someone projects it. If you're feeling weak and insecure, you want someone strong. If you're feeling strong and confident, you might look at someone who appears sensitive to you. In the latter mood, you don't want a brute. You want someone soft, gentle, and caring. On a nonverbal level you pick up the person's gentleness and you feel safe; you know you won't be raped. You allow yourself to be vulnerable.

The husband may have had that chemistry in the first place, but after a while he doesn't show it around the house. He comes home, gets a beer, and sits in front of the TV. He doesn't talk; he grunts at you. All of a sudden you don't see the chemistry. He's got it, all right, but he's not showing it. Soon the attraction begins to wane.

A woman may change and grow more confident and decide she wants another kind of relationship, and her husband isn't willing to change. A marriage has to change and grow. If it doesn't grow, it dies. Marriage is organic. It is the same edict for every living species: "I must grow or die."

M.A.W.: Is it inevitable that people will get bored after years of marriage?

DR. THOMAS: This comes back to how people evaluate themselves. If I rely on external sources to evaluate me, then I'm going to want a new car, a new house, or a new partner. If I am secure within myself, then I don't need the outside sources to tell me who I am. I can live with myself. If a wife allows herself to be herself, she is always changing. Some days she'll be a bitch, or a hooker, some days she'll be shy and retiring. In a sense, every woman is in each woman. If a marriage is such that a woman can feel free enough to let all those different personality traits emerge, and a husband is secure enough to let them emerge, then he's living with a harem.

But if a person is not free, she may feel she has certain things to hide, or that she won't be accepted. Then she begins to hem herself in. She may feel she wants to say something or change something, but she's afraid she'll scare her partner off. She may want a change from the missionary position, but that's the position she's been taught, so that's what she must do, and her husband might think of all the other things he wants to do, but he doesn't share them.

The result is two closed individuals and each one only sees the other in one light. Each has the other in a box, and that's the way it's going to be. Then they look around and see someone else. If they divorce the first person and marry the other, then soon they'll put that second person into a box and get bored.

Boredom doesn't have to set in. If we refrain from putting our spouses in a box, and ourselves in a box, then we don't limit the number of ways in which we can relate. If it's been roast beef every Sunday for twenty years then it's boring. Yet the sad part is that people don't realize their relationship changes all the time. You never cook roast beef exactly the same way every week.

If I can tune into what's happening right now, I'll appreciate the difference. Listening to my feelings and my body is the answer.

The answer isn't out there, it's here, within myself. If I tune into myself, live courageously, and risk letting my spouse see who I am, and my spouse does the same, then we begin to introduce a whole new dimension to our marriage. More and more young people are willing to expose more of themselves to each other, and they are becoming more accepting of their mates.

M.A.W.: Why do middle-aged men have difficulty being open?

DR. THOMAS: In older men there is always conditioning to work against. They feel that, to be a man, they have to be strong and silent and hold back. They hold their feelings back. One man I counselled had lived the image of a swinging bachelor for thirty years, but he wasn't a swinging bachelor. He came in here and we cried together. He said, "Why can't you just hug somebody without someone calling you queer?"

He just wanted to be with someone. He now realizes it's all right to let go of the armor, and he doesn't have to keep up the front. Forty years ago men could show anger, but they couldn't cry or show caring.

If you box someone in, you kill him. Soon he begins to act in the manner in which you define him. That's bad enough, but if you box yourself in, it's psychological suicide. What sometimes happens in a marriage is that you think you want out of the marriage, when what you really want out of is the box.

M.A.W.: What would you suggest couples do to break out of this pattern?

DR. THOMAS: They could start going to growth groups, together or separately. All the growth groups and spiritual movements are positive because they suggest the human animal is opening up the potential to be more gentle, forgiving, and caring.

A couple can begin risking little things like saying, "One of the things I always dreamed of was . . ." They can risk change. If they're always accustomed to buying beer, they can try wine. They should be aware of who they are and change the focus and share the change with their spouse.

Groups are good because they show that other people have the same problems. Even if only one person goes, it will bring about change to both parties. If the wife goes and changes her behavior so she acts in a loving manner, then the husband can't help but change, too. He will have to react differently, so he'll have to change. If she always ordered him about, saying, "Do this, do that!" and she stops, then her husband can't continue to be defensive.

M.A.W.: You're suggesting that what has to change is the way two people interact with each other?

DR. THOMAS: Yes, and you also change your expectations from, "I'm not perfect, but I expect you to be perfect!" The purpose of marriage is helping one's partner to grow and realize his or her potential. It's not expecting to live happily ever after or expecting your spouse always to be there for you and provide for your every need and want.

M.A.W.: Then you must see affairs as threatening to a marriage, since, instead of investing emotionally in the marriage, all the feelings are diverted to someone else and the spouse gets less rather than more?

DR. THOMAS: Yes, if someone becomes more open, free, and total with someone other than the spouse. I don't think affairs are good for marriages, but by the same token, being human, the fact they occur is no reason to end a marriage. Affairs are neither good nor bad. Affairs happen because we're human beings. Very few people plan an affair. If you plan one there is an area of dissatisfaction in your life.

M.A.W.: Do you suggest that people who are having trouble with their marriages should check themselves first?

DR. THOMAS: Yes, they may not be emotionally mature. You are not emotionally mature if you always have to look outside yourself for everything. People who are dissatisfied with their marriages should look at their expectations. They should think about whether the things they're asking for are realistic. If they decide they want to give the marriage a good try, then they should get help.

The worst problem with marriages is people's unrealistic expectations of one another. You can't expect a husband or wife to provide total bliss for you. A spouse can't make you happy, or sad, either. You make yourself happy or sad. Start looking at yourself to see who you are. People don't stop other people from being who they are. It's like the anecdote about the lady who says her husband won't let her work. After he dies, she still doesn't work. She was stopping herself all along. It had nothing to do with her husband.

M.A.W.: Many women tell me they can't picture themselves with the same man for the rest of their lives. How would you explain that attitude?

DR. THOMAS: I think these women have not solved an ego problem. They will keep moving onto somebody else until they begin to take responsibility for their own feelings. They have to recognize that they are responsible for their own sexuality and their own happiness. If they don't take that responsibility, they're going to keep projecting it onto someone else. They must realize they have to look after themselves.

In the following interview, Jean discusses her affair, the reasons it happened, her feelings about it, and her reaction when it ended.

Dr. Thomas has discussed many of the reasons women have affairs. Jean's interview seems to confirm his views.

Jean

Jean is in her early thirties and runs two successful, creative businesses, one in conjunction with her husband, Mark. Jean and Mark have no children. Jean is tall and blond.

I met my first lover in a bar. I was with my friend Sara, who's older and is in the same business I'm in. I had spent a couple of months feeling old and fat. What a combination! I'm only thirty-three, and here I was dragging through life like a tired old bag. Sara and I just went out for a quick drink at this hotel, but there was a dance floor and a band, and we just continued drinking. Sara got up to dance. She's one of those wonderful women from another age: a woman who is independent, yet really loves her husband. Here she was, full of life, while I sat in the corner feeling unattractive. Sara's been married for twenty-five years and she was dancing away with a number of men while I played the old lady. I couldn't stand it. I decided the feelings I had about myself had to change, and I had to take a risk. I wanted to know that I was attractive, but desires like that get you into trouble. On impulse I walked up to an attractive young man at the bar and started talking. I'm in an interesting business, and I felt I could use that as leverage. Well, this man took an immediate liking and interest in me. There was instant rapport. It was as if we belonged together. My husband was forgotten, and I was in another time and place, and this man was mine for whatever length of time we had.

That's one of the things I like best about affairs, being in another time and place, trying another kind of life. I like different possibilities, I like seeing and living the options available. The trouble with being married in this society is that you're confined to one kind of life. And men are dominant. Their space invades yours, and you get into living the life your husband has created for the two of you. Sure, you can create it together, but men usually set the pace. I'm passive in that respect, I guess. Who knows? Anyway, I love leaving my life periodically and jumping into another one. It's fun and refreshing. I like to think it gives me perspective. It's a vacation away from the pressures I've created in my own life. It's better and healthier than drinking away your problems.

My first affair enriched my life in a number of ways. He was fun. We sat down at a table and told stories, laughing all the time as if we were old friends. As I said, there was an attraction, as if we belonged together and were meant for each other. The entire time we were giggling and touching each other. We went up to his room, where we drank rum and Coke and cuddled for a long time. I always feel relaxed and uninhibited after a few drinks. He was gentle, and I was very lucky since he had a huge cock. It was fabulous, just fabulous. I felt filled up. I'm not that large, but my husband doesn't fill me up. It was a friendly fuck. We made love twice and I left about three in the morning. I didn't forget him for months.

My second affair grew out of a friendship. I was in my favorite coffee shop, going over some business papers and talking to the owner of the coffee shop, Michel. I kept complaining flamboyantly about how dull the ideas in the papers were. There was a fellow sitting by himself. He came over and asked me what I was doing. I told him, and we started to talk about my papers. Soon it was dinner time and the coffee shop became busy, so he asked me to go for a walk. He was interested in the subjects I was interested in—philosophy and psychology. I felt mentally stimulated. I felt like a know-it-all, and he doted on me and my every word, as if the words were pearls dropping from my mouth. Jim accepted everything I said, and I do tend to exaggerate. I presented myself very dramatically.

At home I was tired of my husband always talking about his field, a field I know little about. It got so I couldn't hear myself think. I was stifled by my husband, as he took over more and more of my time. I felt powerless because my husband is brilliant. There was a terrific amount of tension when we were working together at first.

We had only started our business and were waiting for our investment to pay off. I felt helpless, just waiting for the business to take off. There were, of course, certain risks involved. You know, most women never know that sense of walking through fear, because usually they've depended for their livelihood on someone else. Most women have no sense of mastery over their own lives. Sometimes all they need to be is cute and loved. As a woman, you can always have drinks, get fed, and have a good time without working at any real job or profession.

But at that point in my life, I was almost suicidal. I needed a vacation, just to check out for a while. I was sick and tired of restrictions and tripping over rules. Rules don't cater to human beings. I needed a rebirth. I believe you can keep your sanity through affairs. Also, that period of time was painful for me. I was tired of criticism, my husband's criticism and the criticism of my friends. I guess I was desperate for fun, as well as for someone who would listen to me. If I'm not fed by someone who listens, then I can't reach out and touch.

Anyway, after leaving the coffee shop, we went for a walk. Jim told me he had been celibate for a long time. I felt a need to take care of him. He was about four years older than I, but his life seemed to be on a detour. I feel most secure at love relationships. There's a feeling of power in knowing you can attract someone. Women like to know they're attractive. I also had lost about sixteen pounds and I felt like a new person. We went running up and down alleys. There was a lot of kissy-touchy stuff. I felt like a crazy lady, which was fun, because I was so tired of being a straight businesswoman. I was overjoyed that Jim was overjoyed at finding such a weirdo. I'm a very physical person, too, and I delight in men. I enjoy the doting part. With men I've always gotten away with murder. I could be so physical with Jim. I felt alive, funny, and more interesting. I had the freedom to feel interesting. Self-discovery also feeds the ego. There's a need to discover other worlds, other parts of yourself. Discovering someone else is fun. Even discovering a new and different body is fun. Jim also really listened, the way shrinks do. Shrinks do get to know your essence.

Nothing happened that night, but when I went home, I felt guilty. I love my husband and what we have in our careers I could never duplicate. I didn't want to jeopardize my marriage. In fact, compared to Jim, my husband looked all the more brilliant. My husband is such a good man; he wouldn't think of doing the same thing to me. Anyway I put Jim out of my mind. About a week later he called and asked me to go to the movies. He's quite a movie buff, and he wanted me to see a certain film. I didn't want to go, so we went for a long walk instead. I wanted Jim, but I was afraid my husband would kill me, so I thought of another woman for Jim. I told him I wanted him, but I couldn't have him. There was an emotional freedom with him because my love was accepted. It was a release from anxiety. I felt Jim treated everything I said with importance.

Finally, I had lunch with the family Jim was living with. Barbara is a widow with two teenaged daughters. Barbara and Jim weren't sleeping together, but Barbara was his friend and she seemed to take up all Jim's time. For two months

Jim and I had lots of lunch dates. It was a good friendship; Jim was always attentive and I was always monopolizing the conversation. It was difficult to do anything else but have lunch—there was no opportunity. Barbara or her daughters were always around, and my husband worked in our office at home.

After about two months, my husband went on a business trip to Los Angeles and Jim came over. We drank. We played and attacked one another for about five hours. It was five hours of foreplay. I love to play rough-house. Eventually, we went to bed. With Jim there were no façades or masks; I felt free to be myself. Anyway, again I was lucky; Jim had a huge cock. It was fabulous; again I felt filled up. I could shower all my attention on him. He's a very sensitive man. I loved the warmth and the closeness of being cuddled. I suppose I was in love with him for a while. I didn't climax and he was disappointed, but I never climax with my husband, either. Jim left about three in the morning. I wanted him again the next day.

Two days later, his girl friend showed up on one of our lunch dates. She was about ten years younger than I am. I didn't feel pretty then. I went berserk.

We didn't make love again. Right now, I need time to work and I can't afford the tension of an affair.

2 Historically Speaking

Sexual mores vary greatly from one culture to another, and from one time period to another within a culture. A brief excursion outside our own culture or period in history can provide an insightful basis for a discussion of sexual attitudes. Or, as the earthy philosopher, Sakini, in *The Teahouse of the August Moon*, put it: "In America . . . statue of nude lady in park win prize. But nude lady in flesh in park win penalty. Conclusion: Pornography question of geography."★

There is no doubt that few modern western women would envy the lives that their counterparts led in sixth-century China. What many might envy, however, was the sexual fulfillment that those women were offered through a philosophy and religion called Taoism. To its adherents, Taoism offered guidelines for all aspects of human life, including sexuality. And since Taoism viewed sexual intercourse as the equivalent of the interaction of cosmic forces, the sex act was a sacred duty that had to be performed often and conscientiously to achieve harmony with Tao, the supreme path.

Since sexual intercourse was one of the main routes to heaven, many detailed and comprehensive sex manuals, with elaborate instructions, soon appeared. These manuals detailed the art of foreplay, intercourse, approved techniques, and

★ John Patrick, *The Teahouse of the August Moon* (New York: G.P. Putnam's Sons, 1952).

positions to enhance sexual enjoyment with specific refer-
ences to the female orgasm. Intercourse was viewed as the
equivalent of the mating of heaven and earth, and the phrase
"clouds of rain" became the standard literary expression for
copulation.

Being true masters of the erotic, the Taoist manuals suggest
delay before penetration. The Jade Stalk was to hover lightly
around the hidden passageway, while the male kissed the
female and teased her Golden Cleft. As her desire increased,
the male was to move to his Positive Peak and hover on the
edge of entry. He was to stroke her breasts and stomach and
then return to the Jeweled Terrace (clitoris). As the woman's
desire increased to fever pitch, he was to move his Positive
Peak back and forth in contact with her Golden Cleft and
Jade Veins (front and back of the vulva). He was to play with
a side-to-side motion on each side of the Examination Hall
(the labia) and finally stop to rest on one side of the Jeweled
Terrace. When the Cinnibar Cleft was in flood and the woman
writhing with expectation, he was to thrust the Vigorous
Peak inward, inserting and withdrawing, moving up and
down. A slow thrust was to resemble the movement of a
carp caught on a hook, while a quick thrust was to be like
"the flight of birds against the wind."

The Flowering Branch brought to the Full Moon (sodomy)
and the Playing of the Flute (fellatio) were permissible as long
as none of the man's "essence" was lost through ejaculation.
Cunnilingus was actively encouraged, as was any other stimulation that increased the woman's "essence."

The manuals suggest some thirty basic positions that increase pleasure and were said, in addition, to cure various
infirmities.

Within Taoist practice, homosexuality was condoned. Po-
lygamy brought large numbers of women together; a middle-
class Chinese male might have as many as three dozen wives
and concubines. The wives were often accompanied by their
relatives and maids; thus lesbianism was common. It has been
noted that the women employed dildos made of ribbed sticks

of wood or specially shaped ivory pieces. Indeed, warnings were issued concerning the excessive use of such tools, which, it was suggested, might harm the delicate tissue within the passageway. Women were also known to utilize a plant called the Cantonese Groin. This plant, which was shaped like the male organ, swelled and hardened when soaked in hot water.

Numerous aphrodisiacs and stimulation devices were also recommended. Men sometimes used rings and tinkling bells. A woman might insert a Burmese Bell within her vagina prior to intercourse. For solitary pleasuring, a pair of silver globes, one containing a drop of mercury and the other a tiny vibrating metal tongue, were employed.

A Chinese wife who followed Taoism did not have to be clever or attractive, but she had to be gentle, orderly, sedate, and discreet. Wives were responsible for being mothers and housekeepers, but were free, within limitations, to spend their time grooming, engaging in lesbian affairs and in illicit relationships with those men they had access to. The rights of every wife and concubine were respected and the husband's duty was to satisfy his wives materially, emotionally, and sexually.

Few other periods in history have given rise to the open eroticism that was so enjoyed during the Taoist flowering. But would today's woman be happy only as slave and sexual partner? The Taoist sexual philosophy is probably appealing only because of the techniques involved in the sexual encounter. The reality of life during this period was, of course, much more difficult. In the end, it is not the life of a Taoist wife in the sixth century that the modern woman envies; it is the suggestion of a sexual technique that recognized the female role and, indeed, catered to it.

In India, where much of life is lived in public, an earthy, open sexuality developed. While lovemaking and speaking about lovemaking was confined to the bedroom in China, this was not so in India.

By the fifth century, Hinduism had influenced all facets of Indian life, including sexuality. The *Kamasutra* was a Hindu manual concerned primarily with sexual technique and the art of flirtation. The *Kamasutra* recognized different types of love and defined love as different from sex. It did, however, recognize that sex was enjoyable and could be made more so by skillfull technique.

The *Kamasutra* emphasized human dimensions and classified the *lingam* (male organ) as a hare, a bull, or a horse. A woman was classified by the size of her *yoni* (vagina) as a deer, a mare, or a cow-elephant. A slightly tight fit was said to make the best union. Numerous suggestions were made and illustrated to assist those with less-than-ideal bodies. Consideration was given to males with small organs, to women with large vaginas, and to those who were especially corpulent. A small organ, for example, might be wrapped in a thin strand of metal or a hollow dildo might be inserted in the woman to make her feel smaller. Assorted salves were also recommended for contracting the vagina temporarily.

The *Kamasutra* was exuberant in its celebration of sex. By the ninth century, devotional cults that dealt strictly with love and sex became popular in India. One of these was Tantra, a cult of ecstasy and joy. Within the cult, sex was considered holy and thought to be a mystical experience. Tantra offered bliss and release from the cycle of reincarnation in one lifetime to those who developed pleasure, vision, and ecstasy. The followers of Tantra argued that if the world was an outward expression of divinity, then everything in it must be divine and worthy of worship. Sexual activity was considered the activity that would lead to a religious, mystical experience. It was said that the oneness of two lovers who were perfectly attuned offered a glimpse of the oneness between the individual and the World Soul. There was emphasis on ritual, temple partners, group sex, and a guru to guide the way.

The devotional cults were dedicated to the joys of sexual pleasure, indeed to the art of pleasuring. Many temples with explicit, elaborate sculptures of couples and groups in various lovemaking postures were built. Sexual enjoyment was highly visible.

Indian and Chinese cultures left many monuments in literature and art praising sexual activity and love; so, indeed, have all Western cultures. But mores in Western societies have tended to be schizophrenic, moving from periods of great permissiveness to periods where any mention of sex was condemned. Judeo-Christianity has also produced societies with parallel sexual standards—one strict, one licentious.

Examples abound. The madonnas of Italian art were usually the mistresses of the painters. More men had mistresses in Victorian England than have them today, and the Victorian period was also one of the great ages of pornography. And even the strictest of Western societies, Puritan New England, was not without its enjoyable pastimes. Good Puritan men and women practised a tradition known as bundling, and indeed, special bundling beds were designed for this purpose. The bed was an ordinary double bed with a board running down the center. Engaged couples were allowed to sleep in the bed for some nights prior to marriage. Sexual penetration was frowned on, but the custom did provide a satisfactory period of foreplay before the wedding night.

When we look at Western societies, it is possible to find examples of women who had affairs in almost every period. Some of these women were condemned, of course, but many were tolerated or even grudgingly admired. Margaret of Valois, for instance, was the wife of King Henry IV of France. A woman of enormous sexual appetite, she had innumerable lovers—among them dukes, generals, and diplomats. Her husband accepted her affairs, probably because he was engaged in illicit relationships of his own. Another famous Frenchwoman, Madame de Pompadour, was the mistress of King Louis XV of France for five years. She was an intelligent and capable woman who enjoyed the king's confidence throughout her lifetime, even after their affair had ended.

The eighteenth-century queen of Spain and consort of King Charles IV, Maria Luisa, was another woman well known for her liaisons with a long succession of dukes, generals, and diplomats. With her favorite lover, Manuel de Godoy, she wielded the real power of government—with unfortunate results. She and Godoy contributed to Spain's downfall at the hands of Napoleon I.

And Napoleon's sister, Pauline Bonaparte, was notorious in her own right for her virtual army of lovers. She was a remarkably beautiful woman who could have her pick of men. But when she was unable to find lasting satisfaction with the nobles, diplomats, and servants of her household, she reputedly took to the streets to invite the first passerby who caught her fancy back to her bedroom. Her promiscuity caused a scandal in a period in French history that was almost as permissive as our own.

Just as affairs were often overlooked or covered up when the woman involved was a member of royalty or nobility, affairs were often tolerated when the woman engaged in them was an actress or writer. Examples of women with active sex lives abound in the artistic community. George Sand, for instance, was a brilliant nineteenth-century French novelist whose many lovers included composer Frederick Chopin. Born Amandine Aurore Lucie Dupin, she scandalized society by changing her name, wearing trousers, and leading a highly unconventional life. Colette was another gifted novelist and lover, who had many affairs with both men and women. To one female lover she is reputed to have written, "My husband kisses your hands, I the rest."

We have no record of how most of these women viewed their affairs. But among women today, there seems to exist one very strong idea, which emerges in interview after interview. It is that sexual activity, even casual sexual activity, must involve love. This elusive word is defined by different women in different ways; sometimes it is not defined at all. Nor is its use a substitute for more descriptive words for sex, which are, in any case, explicit in most interviews. It is clear that women—liberated women, wanton women, dependent women, and women from nearly all walks of life—associate love with sex, and there are strong indications that they think sex must be justified by love. The use of the word *love* for even casual sexual encounters may well indicate the presence of a lingering moralism, the feeling that sex without love must be condemned. It is precisely the same sort of mixed message that one receives from the Bible, which so illustrates our duality of attitude.

Sections of the Bible condemn sexual activity in marriage and outside of it; other sections celebrate sexual enjoyment between mates; the Old Testament commands against adultery, while in the New Testament Christ forgives the prostitute and the fallen woman. One can find many examples of contradictory messages in the Bible about love, sex, and marriage. Since no book has influenced us more, it's perhaps not surprising that we have so many double standards.

It is difficult, if not impossible, to define the culture one lives in with any kind of perspective. We appear to be in a period of sexual openness, but will we return to a period of sexual repression as history suggests we might? Will affairs and all other forms of sexual discussion disappear in a new wave of moralism, leaving only a licentious subculture?

If the sociobiologists are right, the answer to those questions is no. Women can now control reproduction, and while there were always some forms of birth control available to some women, never has so large a population been free of the threat of pregnancy. This is not to say that women do not want children; it is only to say that now they can choose when and by whom they have those children. This knowledge frees a large number of women to enjoy sexual encounters for and in themselves. Women have a new chapter to write in the sexual history of the world.

3 Tina, Nadine, and Elena

Tina

Tina, thirty-eight, lives in Chicago with her husband, Carl.
Carl is an executive with a Fortune 500 company. Tina has
a successful career in advertising. Tina, who is dark com-
plexioned, has black hair, and is pleasingly plump for her
five-foot-six-inch frame. She comes from a middle-class family. She and Carl have no children.

Sometimes I don't know what's wrong with me. I love
men and I need men. My father died when I was ten and I
just can't help myself. I feel for men, which is to say I mother
them. When they're upset or have troubles, I want to soothe
them and care for them. Perhaps that's because I didn't have
a father.

From what I remember, my father was great. He was one
of those dashing young fellows who had it all together. I
especially remember his gold cuff links. I still get off on the
sight of cuff links sticking out of a sleeve. White shirts, well-
tailored suits, and gold cuff links get me hooked before I
know what's happening.

My husband, Carl, is a beautiful man. He's dynamic and

capable. His firm respects him. He looks good and has perfect manners. Actually, I'm quite proud of Carl. When I walk into a restaurant on Carl's arm, we get instant service. It's comforting to know that your husband is looked up to. I feel good about that.

I think my affairs are primarily due to the fact that Carl is seldom home. He gets in at ten after a full day of work, and just drops into bed. He's up again at six. What kind of life is that for me? At first I understood and went back to my own training—the good old Protestant ethic. That did me no good at all. It took me a long time to realize that I wasn't getting everything out of my marriage.

I married at twenty-nine and knew all about men. I already had a successful career in advertising and considered myself to be smart. I can think up ideas quickly. I don't need to spend a lot of time being valuable to my company. For a while I just used my extra time making investments and keeping up with the stock market; I have a golden touch, which I think I inherited from my father.

My affairs started when I was thirty-three. The first man was a lovely, well-dressed fellow who was a single father. I used to see him in the supermarket. One evening we got to talking and he invited me to his place for a few drinks. We spent ten minutes in the parking lot just thinking up excuses for his kids. I got a kick out of that. I enjoy lying once in a while, and the turnaround of having to lie to kids is fun. We got back to his place and spent an hour with his children. His two sons were everything he was, but smaller—charming, fun, and absolutely precocious. We caught up on everything the kids did that day, and he put them to bed. He even offered to let me read them their story. I don't have any children and it was a pleasure for Tina to watch this man with his offspring. Once the kids were in bed the night was ours. I called home and left word with my answering service that I had to work late. I knew I was ready for an affair.

It didn't take us long to realize that we had something going. By the way he looked at me, I knew he had a real need for me. His wife didn't want children, she wanted her career, and so he wound up with the kids. His story was too much; it brought back old longings to have children. We talked for a long time, he about his frustrations with work, and me about Carl. I began to realize how much I was missing in life.

Carl could provide for me like no other man I could imagine. He could be sensitive, caring, and generous. That part of me that demands to be treated as special was fully satisfied by my husband. But I crave affection from him in public to show people that I am loved. For Carl, affection is a private act; he's not a passionate man.

This first affair lasted about three months. We got together after work, had a few drinks, put the kids to bed, then got in the sack ourselves. The affair ended when one of the kids asked me if I was going to be their new mommy. That was a bit too much of a shock for me. The kids seemed too attached to me, and their father began to realize that his kids wanted a mother, not Aunt Tina.

My second affair started at an el [subway] station. In my single days, I would dream about cracking the fine art of picking up someone at an el station. The elevated stations in Chicago are not the best places for pickups, but still it was something I always wanted to do. I see myself as quite the rebel sometimes, and rules are made to be broken, the more the merrier. Anyway, here's this man reading his newspaper on the platform and I start asking him some ridiculous questions, like "How many people got zapped today?" or something equally stupid. I like being playful, and the news as it exists today lends itself to slapstick.

This guy turned out to be okay. He was surprised that anyone would have the nerve to speak on an el platform to a stranger. Chicago just isn't one of those cities where people feel comfortable speaking with each other on the transit system. We started talking. He enjoyed my openness and asked me to join him for a drink. We didn't even wait for a train. We literally ran out of the station to a bar. We talked and talked. He wasn't married and that was great. He was truly interested in my work and asked a lot of questions without making any asinine comments about how awful advertising people are, and how we're responsible for all the ills in society. Suddenly he started to come on to me, talking about how he had to fuck me. There was no other way around it.

Hardly anyone tells me I'm fabulous anymore. Carl will only say the right words on social occasions. I need to hear I'm beautiful and desirable much more often. Anyway, this guy starts whispering about how much he wants me. Men who love women and really want them are difficult to turn down.

He insisted on taking me back to his apartment. He was making me laugh with his lines—"I can't stand being with you without fucking you" or "Your scent is driving me crazy." I started to get into it as well. We began playing and I slipped my hand under the table and rubbed him until he was stiff. He was turning every color of the rainbow, and we never stopped laughing. It was hard to leave the bar. He was sticking out all over the place, and trying to get his member to relax, and I kept making moves to keep it hard.

Finally we had to leave. These games we were playing were getting to both of us. There was no question in either of our minds—we just had to fuck and quickly. Eric took some money out of his wallet and paid the bill, and tried calmly to walk out of the bar with me on his arm. It was impossible. Every time I saw that bulge in his pants, I began to giggle.

We got back to his place and started going at it hot and heavy. He dived for me. He wouldn't even wait for me to get my pantyhose off. That man's tongue never stopped. After he had gone down on me, we got into some neat fucking. He knew how to work at it and get in deep, which I just adore. I lost count as to the number of times I came, and we were both exhausted.

I must have arrived home around three in the morning.

Carl was fast asleep and I showered quickly. I was so afraid that my husband would pick up the scent of sex.

I began calling Eric constantly and turning him on over the phone. It became my morning and afternoon game. He loved it. The affair lasted almost a year—until I realized he was seeing three other women. I don't know how I found out; it's something you almost realize intuitively. Nothing to go on, just the odd little thing, like the wrong color hair in the brush, things like that. I couldn't really question him about it, but I started feeling cheap. I was afraid that I would get VD or something. There's much that I can explain to Carl, and there are also areas that I would rather not face. VD is one of them.

I was feeling dirty. After a while I just let the whole thing fizzle out. I'm too good to be treated like everyone else. Carl taught me that. Why should I risk VD? No way! I never stick around when someone is getting me down.

I'm having an enjoyable affair right now with a fellow named Joe. Joe isn't everything I want, but he is a good complement to Carl. Joe is just . . . well . . . down to earth. Nothing to write home about, but perfect at being himself. He's not elegant, but I'm never seen in public with him, anyway. Joe is foreman at a factory and quits at five. We can be together from five to ten every night when we want to. Joe doesn't pressure me; when I'm tired or want a night alone he understands. When I need him, we can go to bars, or to his place to just play. We like talking, and we're learning a lot from each other. We make a good team. I'll never leave Carl for Joe. Each of my men fills a special need in me.

I doubt seriously whether one man can ever fully satisfy my needs. I'm too complicated, and my needs are too varied. Most men I know are good in any number of ways, but not in all ways. With Carl I can share an elegance, and with Joe there is that warm down-to-earth feeling. There will never be anyone out there who will fill all my needs.

Nadine

Nadine is thirty-two years old and works in a high-technology plant in the suburbs of Toronto. She is the first person in her family in the last three generations to have a full-time job that has lasted more than five years. She comes from a working-class background.

Frank and I were married in 1975, and I really believed that he was the man for me. I slept around a bit before we got married, but all that was back home in New Brunswick. In any case, none of those flings was serious. I wasn't the town tramp or anything like that.

Right after we got married, Frank and I moved to Toronto, but the job market being what it was, I got work and Frank didn't. It took Frank more than two years to find work. It hurt him badly, and it didn't help our marriage any. We both believed that we left our pasts behind, and anything we wanted to do we could do. After all, there was one pay check coming in, and the unemployment insurance Frank was pulling in made it the most money we ever had in our lives. Still, Frank needed to work, otherwise he'd be hanging around the bars from their opening until I got home.

Those first two years in Toronto were sheer hell. Frank just couldn't take it. He was drinking more than he ever had before, and once he hit me, not hard, really, but damn it, he hit me. And no one, I mean no one, ever hit me except my dad. Around the same time, Frank started staying out late. He'd come home reeking of booze, and I was positive he was playing around. I was furious. There I was paying the rent, buying the groceries, paying most of the bills, and Frank was using his unemployment money to go out drinking and have himself a good old time. Either he was getting loaded or he was getting laid, and the result was I got nothing.

I never gave much thought to playing around after I got married. I was raised a Catholic, and you just don't do that kind of thing. Frank might be a pain in the neck, but he was my husband and I kept thinking that once he got some work it would be okay.

Anyway, one day at the plant a new supervisor took over my department. He was a really good-looking guy from Montreal. He reminded me of Burt Reynolds. I always had a crush on Burt Reynolds. I found out soon after he started that he was married and that his wife, who was still in Quebec, was closing up their place. It was plain after just a few days that he was lonely as hell.

By the end of the first week, we got to talking a lot to each other, mostly during our breaks. It was really strange. We both liked the same movies, television shows, and magazines. Once Pete and I would get to talking, it took the factory whistle to make us remember where we were. The second week Pete asked me to join him for a drink after work. I felt like a high-school kid; I mean no one ever asked me out for a drink. What impressed me most was Pete's almost-shy attitude. I didn't know who was more afraid that night—me or Pete. The warmth and good feeling we would have on our breaks was practically gone at this bar. We were really up-tight.

When I got home that night—it must have been around ten—Frank wasn't home yet. About an hour later he came barreling in as he usually did, drunk as a skunk. We made love that night and all I could think about was Pete. Every time Frank touched me, I told myself it was Pete. When Frank was rough, I knew Pete would be gentle. It was really strange; it had to be the best and the worst sex I ever had. Frank was a total pig that night. In the past Frank and I made love, but that night he just fucked me. If he wasn't so goddamn lazy, he could have used his hand for the satisfaction he gave me. Still, in my mind, I imagined it was Pete who was making love to me. He was tender and loving and we climaxed together. When we finished, we just held each other closely.

All that night as I lay awake next to Frank, I couldn't stop thinking of Pete and how it could be with someone who is special.

The next morning, when I got out of bed, I was determined that Pete and I would get together. When the coffee break came, I cornered Pete and got up my courage to ask him out to dinner. Where I grew up girls just didn't do that. Damn it, though, I was lonely. Pete was kind of taken aback, but he agreed.

There was this Italian restaurant I had been trying to get Frank to take me to for months. Pete and I went there that night. It was beautiful. The waiter brought the wine that Pete ordered, and Pete tasted it and nodded to the waiter. It was just like a movie. Throughout the meal, I took every opportunity to touch him—under the table, of course. Wow! He touched me back. It was exactly like I had dreamed it would be the night before. He was gentle, kind, everything that Frank used to be, but was no longer.

It didn't matter that the restaurant lacked a violin player going from table to table; I heard violins anyway. I was taken into a world that I knew was mine, a world that was filled with love and tenderness. I didn't want the evening to end, and, to my joy, Pete wanted the evening to last. I was going crazy. I was afraid that Pete wouldn't ask me back to his place or something like that. I was tempted, myself, to ask him, but fortunately he wasn't as shy as I thought. My biggest problem was saying yes too quickly.

Pete was staying at a motel on the outskirts of Toronto, and that's where we wound up that night. If I wasn't so hungry for Pete, it would have been funny. This was the first time in my life that I had been in a motel with a man. Pete fumbled with the key to the door for what seemed like eternity, and finally we were inside the room.

Well, without getting into too many details, making love with Pete was fantastic. I felt like it was the first time all over again. I was a silly high-school girl with a crush on the captain of the football team. We kissed, we touched. I mean we touched. There were parts of my body that my husband had ignored for as long as we knew each other. We must have made love about three times that night.

It could have gone on forever, but the phone rang. From Pete's tone of voice, I knew it was his wife. He stammered a lot, and kept talking about how tired he was, and what a long day it had been. But the mood was broken, as I guess it had to be eventually. As I told you earlier, I'm a Catholic, and there is no place in my world for divorce. I was feeling guilty enough just being with another man, let alone having it lead to a divorce.

We didn't say much to each other after he hung up the phone. I quietly put on my clothes, and Pete put on his. When we got into his car and he began driving me back to my car, he mentioned that his wife would finally be coming in a week. He had to start looking for a house. We arrived back at the restaurant parking lot, and we kissed each other good-night.

Thank God Frank was asleep when I got home. It must have been close to one in the morning. Even if he was awake, chances were he was so drunk that he wouldn't even know his own name, let alone the hour I came home. Still, the next morning I felt really awful, not sick or anything like that, just troubled. Frank was still sleeping when I left for work, so fortunately I didn't have to deal with him that morning. I went to church that day. I was too ashamed to even talk to the priest. I sat in the back of the church and prayed.

I don't know if I got any answers that day, but I went home to Frank. For a change he was home, and even more surprising, he was stone-cold sober. He had been out looking for work and was really happy about some promising leads he had picked up. We didn't talk at all about the previous night, but I suspect Frank knew. You don't know someone for as long as we've known each other and not be sensitive to their feelings. Surprisingly, Frank was being supportive and kind. He was the Frank I fell in love with and married.

Frank still doesn't know for sure about that night. I never

had another affair. I was too nervous and, besides, life was a lot better at home. Frank finally got himself a job, and Pete's wife occupied all of Pete's time.

The affair I had with Pete was a kind of life preserver. I was sinking fast. Before Pete, I was starting to feel like the man of the house. Pete made me feel like a woman again. I'm sure Frank saw the change. My change, I believe, brought about a change in Frank, and it was for the better.

Elena

Elena is twenty-six years old. She is well-built, five-feet-five inches tall with long brown hair and bright brown eyes. She claims to be "only a housewife." She is married to Tom, who is the vice-president of a multinational firm. Elena has two young children. Her background is middle-class.

I've only had one affair, but it's lasted now for eleven years. In fact, I lead a double life. I've been happily married to Tom now for four years, but have never been able to give Steve up. I haven't even tried.

I was fifteen when I met Steve and we fell in love. We went to school together and were a steady couple. We went to college together as well and spent four more years as inseparable friends and lovers. We both studied the same subject—sociology—and so we even took the same classes. I, and everyone else, always assumed I'd marry Steve, and when we planned to live together in Montreal my mother began to plan our wedding because it seemed we were so right for each other.

Steve and I lived together for six months after we left school. It was then I realized this man would never marry. Every time I mentioned the children we'd have, he clammed up. He really couldn't handle it.

One night Steve had some sort of nightmare and woke up tossing around mumbling, "Marriage, children, it's no good, they'll get hurt." Things like that. I asked Steve about his dream in the morning and he didn't have the vaguest idea what I was talking about. Soon after that, we started to fight over the silliest incidents. Steve would stand over me when I was cooking and complain about the way I fried eggs. And he'd leave for work without even kissing me good-bye. Our lives went from bad to worse, and one day Steve said, "Find someone else. I don't want you around here anymore!"

I cried for weeks, and one day when I was in the park Tom sat down to talk to me. I'd seen him at a party at a friend's house the Saturday before. Even though I was broken up about Steve, I kept dragging myself out to these parties.

Tom and I talked for a while, and he asked me to go for a drink with him, and I did, thinking it would cheer me up. It did.

Tom is very charming and full of fun. He had me laughing all evening and I realized I could be happy with someone else, especially with Tom.

Tom and I started to see each other regularly. Tom had money, he had a good job at the time and was always given the best raises, and he'd get fat bonuses for the spectacular deals he was able to make. Steve was an odd-job man; he owned his own small business and never could take me out. Being with Tom was all new to me, and being treated splendidly with flowers, jewelry, and dinners excited me.

Steve promoted my relationship with Tom, insisting he still loved me but that Tom was better for me. One day, Tom asked me to marry him. Steve was thrilled. All the pressure was off him to marry me and he went back to being just lovable Steve. He even picked out my wedding dress. It was that silly.

Steve had moved to Andrea's house and left me with the apartment we had shared, so I could see Tom there. Tom really believed then, and still believes, that Steve is Andrea's boy friend. Andrea's a lesbian and she has always covered for Steve and me. We cover for her, too, with her parents and colleagues, so it all works out well.

Tom and I had a beautiful wedding and Steve was all smiles. My mother was in tears—she wanted me to marry Steve and really couldn't cope with what was going on. She barely knew Tom: she liked him, but he wasn't "her Steve." Steve is one of those men who light up older women's lives with charming lines.

Tom and I had a wonderful honeymoon in Barbados and we developed a fairly good sex life. It took some time because Tom is sexually inhibited. He prefers the old missionary position, and I really have to work hard getting him to overcome his sexual fears. We got our sex down to a warm, cuddly closeness and I've finally realized that that's all I can expect from Tom. Tom loves me dearly, I know that, and I know he's the best husband I could have.

After the wedding and honeymoon, Steve started to come over now and again when Tom wasn't home, and he started to make love to me again. It was as natural as can be and neither one of us felt any guilt.

Ever since I was sixteen I've been making love to Steve and so it just sort of continued, marriage or no marriage. Steve is a dynamite lover; he takes his time with me and knows my body well. He was the one I had my first climax with and through the years we've known each other, Steve has helped me get to know my own body. We used to cuddle up and read all the sex manuals together and then we'd try out all the techniques. Years ago, we spent a holiday weekend trying out all the positions in the *Kamasutra*. We had about twenty more positions to try, but we were both exhausted and my cunt hurt! See, when someone knows you as intimately as Steve knows me, it's impossible to give him up, absolutely impossible. With Steve I feel that every inch of me is known and every inch is loved. After oral sex with Steve, I feel pure and whole and all together. There's no feeling of dirtiness or rejection; I love my whole body and it feels good.

Steve's body is heaven to me, too. I love the smell of his sweat and I know and love every hair around his penis. That's the way it is with Steve and one of the reasons neither of us has any guilt about loving each other even though I'm married.

Tom can never know about my relationship with Steve because it would kill him. Tom really believes that I'm radiant and happy because he makes love to me so well. How could I tell him it's not him? I can't tell him it's Steve who makes me that way. Tom is delighted with me and adores me. All his friends believe he must be the greatest lover in the world because I look so well screwed. I have that look of a sexually satisfied woman, while the wives of Tom's friends look frustrated and unhappy. My mother even gives Tom the credit and envies me for my good luck.

Even when I was pregnant, Steve made love to me at least three or four times a week and it was heavenly. I walked around with a huge belly, looking satisfied and contented.

Having babies—I have two—made me feel feminine and Steve loved it. As long as he wasn't responsible for the children he was happy as could be and continued to love me. Our love is still growing; I don't think it will ever die.

Tom is taking more and more business trips these days because he is moving up in the firm, and he appreciates the fact that Steve and Andrea come over to play with the kids and keep me company. Little does he know what's going on.

The only problem I've ever had with this affair is the fear that the children will look like Steve. Both Steve and Tom are tall with brown hair and brown eyes, so it really never concerned me too much. But Deborah's eyes are beginning to look a little too much like Steve's. Steve has this special glint that's unique to him and it makes me nervous. I try not to worry about it, but every once in a while this terror strikes.

Andrea's career sometimes makes me nervous, too. As long as Tom thinks that Andrea and Steve are together, Tom won't worry about my seeing Steve alone. If they broke up, we'd have to work out a new plan of action. Recently, Andrea was asked to move to Vancouver by her company and I prayed she wouldn't accept the job. She didn't, thank God.

I believe the fates, as I call them, have been good to me and continue to be good to me. I feel very blessed. It's like the sun keeps shining on me.

4 Claudia, Cindy, and Darlene

Claudia

Claudia is forty-eight. She is an artist who has been married twice and is currently separated. She has raised two children of her own, and three stepchildren. Her background is upper-middle-class. She lives in Vancouver.

Affairs are fun—a form of recreation that is entertaining and needn't be tacky. They remind me of eating chocolate pudding. I enjoy myself. I especially enjoy attention. I think any woman who said she didn't enjoy attention would be a liar.

I had many affairs during both my marriages. I considered affairs as a separate world—a world apart from husband and wife. All the responsibility for a house, children, and a husband is not really me. I was always more of a free spirit. Affairs were a way to be myself and be accepted as just a woman. Sex was never the main reason for an affair; I never had any complaints about my mate. It was more that affairs were a way to be judged for myself alone and to see if I was acceptable. When you first meet a man who is a stranger, he has to take you as you are. You have to be you. He doesn't have the benefit of knowing about your parents and your family. In an affair I was judged for myself alone and I had a chance to find out if I was really me, and not just a shadow of all the people who raised me. The affair was the reassurance that I was okay as myself. My first husband's family and my family were friends, and when we married, I felt I was judged acceptable because of my parents' influence.

My other reason for having affairs was the wild side of my personality. I consider myself a gentle person who doesn't do dangerous things like climb mountains, but there is a side of me that enjoys doing something risky. The danger in affairs is the fear of being caught. Living on the edge of that fear is exciting. In my imagination I weave an exciting scenario. Affairs tend to make people think someone is dying for sex, but I don't believe sex was the biggest attraction. There were many other reasons.

My first affair started before I was married and continued for several years after I was married. It was romantic and not sexual. The man I worked for wrote me long love letters daily. We would meet in strange places to talk, usually the graveyard. The graveyard has always been my favorite place to meet people because there is never anyone there. In fact, I've made love in many strange and funny places. One fellow I had an affair with drove a Cadillac with a vinyl roof. One night we were parked off the main road. He was afraid that people might see us when their car lights flashed through the window. I suggested we climb on the roof because no one would think of looking there. As I climbed up, I could feel the roof buckling, and all I could think of was the fact we were going to destroy his beautiful car. But we made love on the roof with all the cars passing. It was just great—all the stars were out.

During another affair I was driving home with my lover when I said to him, "Stop the car! I just have to make love right away!" We pulled off onto a side road. I told him no one would see us. At the height of activities, a school bus came down the road and stopped in front of the car. All the kids got off and waved to us.

Another fellow with whom I had an affair was a skeet shooter. One day when we went to the shooting range, I walked ahead of him and started taking off my clothes one by one. He couldn't believe I'd do this. I still have the piece of clay pigeon that was embedded in my back. He told me he could never shoot skeet there again. He kept getting foul scores because all he could see was me peeling off my clothes.

I used to think ladies who had affairs weren't moral, but I consider myself a proper person. I never thought I was hurting anyone since I've always been good friends with my lovers after. I justified my affairs because I always believed if anything felt good, a person should do it. If you know what makes you tick, you should do it; you're ahead of the game. I think it is vital to know yourself, and people should be true to themselves first. I enjoy affairs, and they make my life enjoyable. Affairs are healthy and a great way to keep in shape mentally and physically.

I never let myself feel guilty or cheap because of the affairs. I think if you do feel guilty, it shows on your face and you look hardened.

Some of my affairs lasted several years. I've also had two or three at a time. I suppose each one of my lovers knew of the others, although they never said anything to me. One-night stands were quite a different thing. I can't even remember some of those men. I simply took what I wanted from them, and I never felt used.

The affairs never broke up my marriages. Neither husband had any idea I had affairs, and neither was unfaithful to me. They weren't the disloyal type. I loved my two husbands very much and they have become good friends. We had great relationships. I know that I didn't hurt my husbands. Differences came up in the marriages and I started nagging and picking at little habits. I don't like women who nag, and I felt if I stayed I would have made two people unhappy. I thought it was time to get out and move on to something different. My first marriage lasted ten years, my second lasted twelve, although I felt I had stayed two years too long. Since I didn't make my second marriage work, either, I feel I'm not really marriage material.

My most exciting sexual adventures have happened in the Caribbean. Something happens to me there: I get island fever. One time when I was in Nassau on a vacation, I screwed more guys than I ever have. There must have been five in one week. My husband couldn't figure out why I lost twelve pounds, and the girl friend who went with me didn't know how to explain to her husband why she was so tanned and I was so pale. The pace was so hectic that I remember finding a pair of shoes under the couch and I couldn't remember who to give them to. One man would leave and another one would come in.

The affairs in Nassau started the first night I was there. My girl friend went out and I was feeling rather lonely. There was a band playing in the lounge and I went down and stood in the doorway to listen to them. A very young, good-looking fellow came over and asked me to join his group of friends. There were a number of young girls at the table. Chris, the young man who invited me over, asked me if I'd like to go outside where it was quieter. When we got outside, he put his arm around me. I couldn't believe it because I was twice his age. We made love that night, and he came up several times to visit me afterwards.

I spotted another fellow out of the window of my room. He was sitting beside the pool with his wife and another couple. I grabbed my girl friend and we went down and played Ping-Pong near them. His wife was quite jealous. He met me on the rocks by the beach and ended up spending most of the night in my room. He told his wife he had fallen asleep on the billiard table downstairs. He kept coming all week and getting into all sorts of trouble with his wife.

I also met a cute young fellow who helped me fix my foot when I cut it on coral, but he was just a quickie.

Near the end of the week I met this marvelous, handsome

man. I saw him at the pool and I walked by him several times to get his attention. He asked me out to dinner. There were several attractive, wealthy women at the table and I couldn't figure out what he was doing with me. He spent the next two and a half days with me. He was so handsome I didn't dare get to know him, because I thought I could really fall for him. The last day I was screwing him in the shower when my plane was about to take off. I dumped all my clothes into my suitcase and ran downstairs with my hair dripping wet.

Anyhow, I have had many affairs and when I run out of men, I'll start on women.

Cindy

Cindy is forty-five. She is into the third year of her second marriage. She has five children from her former marriage and two stepchildren from her current marriage. She is petite and pretty. She is working as a secretary and taking classes at business school. She and her second husband live in St. Paul, Minnesota. Her background is small-town and middle-class.

I first married when I was eighteen to a boy of eighteen, after going steady and sleeping with him for four years. We used to sneak off and make love. I wasn't interested in school, although I was a good student. I was young and in love and wanted to be married. This boy was attractive, amorous, and ambitious. I needed a lot of affection because I was an only child and adopted: I rather resented the fact that I was adopted. My parents were overly strict and completely undemonstrative. Although I knew they were in love with each other, they never openly showed their affection for each other or for me. I wanted friends and companionship.

My parents were upset by my marriage. They were both

professional people and wanted me to finish my education. I now regret not having gone further in school. I feel as if I messed up my life by marrying so young. Getting married was the thing to do in those days, and here I was with a handsome boy in love with me. No one could tell me differently; I had to learn by doing. My mother told me that I had made my bed, and now I must lie in it. I knew I could never turn to her if I had any problems.

After the wedding, things changed almost immediately. Claude suddenly didn't like all the activities I thought he enjoyed. He didn't like swimming, picnics, or my friends. He had girl friends right from day one. This lasted for the entire thirteen years of our marriage. With Claude I was always pregnant, barefoot, and in the kitchen. I always thought another child might help. It didn't, and I ended up with five children. I was left to raise the children; Claude was never interested in them. He was also terrible with money, so there was always financial strain. He was a smart man, but very immature and always after a new conquest.

I lived with little or no love for most of the marriage; however, I continued to love Claude and to believe he would change. I stayed because I was raised not to give up, or divorce, or have affairs. People talked about people who did those things. I was in a quandary. I thought, "What do I do about the kids? What do I do about me? What do I do about my life?" I had no education, and I'd never had a job. To leave with all those children would be a gigantic step. I tried to hang on and make things work.

My husband got a job in Denver, about two hundred miles from the town where we lived. He didn't want me to move down with him. He came home when he felt like it, which was about every third or fourth weekend. I felt lonely and unloved, and I knew he was playing around in the city. We had no sex life. He started to flaunt his latest girl friend in front of me. Then he took her to meet his parents. I knew the marriage was over. We had almost signed separation papers two years after the marriage, but didn't. Even a few months after our wedding, one of my mother's friends had told her I didn't look happy. But I couldn't go home.

I guess the kids kept me going for a long time; they were an outlet for love and affection. Finally I got a job while Claude was in the city. It gave me some kind of independence. I was planning to end the marriage. My husband didn't really care what I did.

I found work in a dentist's office. The dentist and I became good friends. I enjoyed all the attention he gave me. It was more than I had had in fifteen years of marriage.

I became infatuated. I needed someone to care about me; my husband didn't. The dentist was unhappily married, but I knew there was no way out for him. However, you always hope something will come out of it. We became lovers, and he was a super lover. It was fun and exciting. I didn't feel guilty because I knew my marriage was over. It was safe, too, because I didn't really need anything more than love-making at the time. I thought he was someone who cared, but I realized afterward that sex isn't necessarily caring. He told me I needed someone who cared more about me than I cared about him. The affair lasted three months.

At the end of the affair, my husband and I decided to get a divorce. I took the two youngest kids and he took the three older ones. I got another job, but I found it almost impossible to work as well as raise the kids. I had a difficult time coping. Five years after we separated, my husband asked me to come back to him. He needed someone to look after the children, even if it was me. I said no.

After a few years and a few other men, I met a man I loved. A girl friend and I were at a bar, and she knew this man and introduced me. We hit it off. John had been widowed a few months earlier. He was a professional man, and influential in the community. He was twenty years older than I was. He appealed to me because he cared. He was a pillar in the community, well-liked, and he had lots of money. I helped him with his teenage children and they liked me. We saw each other every day. He offered me security, a good life, and decent friends. When he moved—about four hundred miles away—he asked me if I would move, too. We maintained separate places, but saw each other often.

Finally, he retired. He had quite a bit of money. He asked me to go traveling with him. I thought perhaps this would lead to marriage. My two kids went to live with their father, and we left for warmer climates. We toured all over the south and Mexico in high style, meeting many new people and seeing new places. We rented a house on one of the islands for a year. His kids and my kids visited us. It was an experience few people ever get. After a few years, however, I wanted to get married. He told me he would never marry again. I couldn't believe it. I thought he loved me. He told me he still loved and missed his wife, although he cared for me. Although life was good, something was missing.

We settled in a house in California overlooking the ocean. Our life became what he wanted. Age caught up with him. He took many afternoon naps, and our life became inactive, except for the occasional round of bar-hopping. It was hard to get him going. Life became boring. I just couldn't sit around all day and do nothing. I think I still would have married him, if he had asked. His needs at his age were so much different than mine. I knew John cared about me in his own way, but it wasn't enough for someone my age. I had been with him eight years.

I had been separated nine years, and I had a lot of time to think about what I wanted and where I was headed. You learn a hell of a lot. I had gained in experience and age. I knew what I wanted out of life. I wanted someone who liked the same activities I do, someone who needed love as I do. Age broadens your horizons; it helps you to understand the past. Sometimes people grow away from one another. You find something you like to do and the other person isn't interested. I always thought that there was something new to learn every day. I think there are never enough hours in the day to do all I want to do. Anyone who gives up learning and doing has given up on life.

Once again I left a man. I went back up north and got a job and an apartment. I don't think John really knew why I left. He came and asked me to go back down south with him, but by this time, I had already met the man who became my second husband. I knew by then that I needed a man closer to my own age who cared about a home and a family, a man who was interested in life. By this time, I was strong and independent. Sometimes I think I may be too independent. I knew when I left that there had to be someone, somewhere who was right for me. You have to be strong when you have kids, because some of the things they put you through can be heartbreaking, but you can survive.

A friend introduced me to Wayne, my second husband. She had gone out with him, but decided that although he was attractive he was not her type and he was too old for her. Wayne and I hit it off right away. He took me out for supper, dancing and to a party that night. We had so much fun that I knew right away he was the one. I wanted him and that was all there was to it. He loved children and animals, and he wanted a home. We went out constantly from the time we met. Our only regret was that we didn't meet each other twenty years earlier. He was stable and had his life in order, and I knew he wasn't going to change after we got married as my first husband had. He cared, really cared.

We were married and now after three years, every day is just like the day we were married. We work hard to keep it that way, and to be caring and sexy for one another. Sex is important to marriage. It's not the most important aspect, but if you've got sexual problems, you've got marital problems. He's thoughtful and considerate. If I've had to work late, he'll have supper ready for me when I come home. On my birthday, he sends me roses at the office. Each anniversary is like a honeymoon. We go to a hotel and have a wonderful, exciting time. He's thoughtful, and we make a point of spending time with each other alone. I can't believe I'm so lucky and married to such a wonderful man.

I think communication is the biggest factor in a relationship. If you can't communicate with your mate, you're really lost. I don't think being married means you have to cling to each other. You can each be individuals. There's room for freedom of choice. I'm taking new courses at school, and my husband is encouraging me. The courses make me feel good about myself. They make me feel as if I can contribute and build a career. I had a good start in life, but I messed it up from the beginning.

Anyway, I'm happier now than I've ever been, but it took a long time, and years of experience, to create that happiness.

Darlene

Darlene is fifty. She is blond and looks much younger than she is. She is divorced. She raised her children on her own, and she now has a career in journalism, which allows her to travel a great deal. She has not remarried. After her divorce, she returned to university and moved away from her home town.

Looking back, I can't believe I was the dull and naive person I used to be. My first affair was wonderful—exciting and terrifying at the same time. It was a learning experience for me sexually, as well as in other ways. Once I got over my terror and finally made love to Douglas the first time, I could hardly wait until I saw him again. What he taught me about making love, hugging, kissing, holding and satisfying your partner would fill a library. It was marvelous and I have since branched out in my sex life.

My affair taught me about myself and showed me there were choices. I learned there was much more to life and loving than what I was getting at home. I had always considered my marriage the norm. My affair taught me better. I can remember how terribly naive I was about sex and marriage.

I was in my thirties when a friend of mine got a divorce. No one in my circle had got divorced and no one in my immediate family had done it either. My friend dated a man for about six months. Later, when she told me what a great lover this man was, I was flabbergasted. It had never occurred to me that she was sleeping with him. Of course, I had no idea what "a great lover" was at that time. My husband was the only man I had ever gone to bed with. In the fifties and sixties men didn't care if they satisfied you or not. My husband had a problem with premature ejaculation. I learned to come the minute he entered because it was the only way I could get any satisfaction. That experience proved to be a bonus. Today, that's why men like me. I always come. Men get discouraged if they can't make a woman come. Somewhere along the way every woman should have a great lover to show her what works.

It was definitely the problems in my marriage that led me into the affair. While I was married I didn't feel there was really a me. I wasn't good; I wasn't bad; I wasn't wonderful. I was just there, doing what I was supposed to do—cleaning, cooking, and having babies. In those days when people introduced me they would say, "She's kind, she's generous, and she's sweet." Never would anyone say, "She's fun to be with and she's interesting." I was just placid and noncontroversial. Today someone will introduce me as a terrific gal and a great person. I can't imagine how boring I must have been.

I got married at nineteen. I was brought up in a fundamentalist environment in the midwest where everything was considered bad. When I got married, it was to be permanent. About three weeks after we were married, I was lying on the couch with my husband, and I started kissing him very tenderly and gently. I was not experienced sexually, so I was experimenting. He said, "Stop that! It sexes me up too much." I never kissed him again unless he initiated it.

My husband's job as an accountant kept him away from home for long hours, and also out of town for weeks at a time. Looking back, I feel there was little substance to the marriage. We had sex every two or three weeks, when he would be home for a weekend. I thought that was normal. I never looked at or thought about other men. As far as I know, he was faithful.

I received little attention from my husband. He considered himself a good provider and he worked extremely hard. He did little at home. Gradually I began to grow up. Later, when all the children were in school, I was allowed to take a course at college. It kept me young and active. One day a radical acquaintance told me I had choices in life. I didn't understand what she was talking about. I had been complaining about my sex life, which had dwindled to nothing over the years. I was complaining about my lack of money. Working was not allowed. I complained that my husband threatened to take the car away because of something I had done.

The lack of sex continued for three years. One year my husband was out of town for a total of eight and a half months. He made love to me once in all of that year. Each year I would ask him to ask the doctor what was wrong. I couldn't discuss it with our GP; I was filled with terror at the thought of bringing the subject up. My husband would report that the doctor had said he was working too hard. I'd go to the same doctor and he'd give me tranquilizers so I wouldn't cry myself to sleep.

My husband started wearing his shorts and a T-shirt under his pajamas. If I ever dared to touch him, he would giggle nervously and say, "Stop that!" The last few times he did make love to me, he ejaculated prematurely. He entered me with no foreplay. Truly, I was being driven crazy.

After my friend explained to me what she meant by saying I had choices, I finally began to think there might be more to life than I was getting.

The beginning of the end of the marriage came one Sunday afternoon when one of the kids wrecked the Venetian blind and my husband, in a fury, said, "I'll never buy you a new couch now. You don't deserve it!" I was miserable. Later that day we went to a party, which was being thrown for a winning football team. As we walked in, I was still feeling hurt, anger, disbelief, and I thought to myself, "I have to divorce him." I was afraid I couldn't support myself and the children. I had no marketable skills.

About a half an hour later, I walked by an enormous black football player. He said to me, "You're really unhappy. What can I do to help? I saw you walk into the hall and something has really upset you!" I was overwhelmed. Here was a man who had noticed something about me and seemed to care.

We talked for quite a while. I told him some of my problems and he said he'd like to help me, either by showing me how to make my husband happier or perhaps by showing me how to get what I wanted from him. I agreed to let him call me.

The next day he called and we agreed to meet in his car outside my classroom at college. We talked for two hours the first day. He met me every day and we talked. He was so sympathetic, so kind, so understanding, and gradually so wonderful that I began to find him sexually attractive. He began kissing me hello and good-bye, then we started necking, and after a couple of weeks we started steaming up the car. One day he took me to his friend's house, but his friend wasn't there. I didn't make love with him that day because I was still too terrified, but he realized he was bringing me around. He was a very sensitive person. The next time we were alone I was very tense, but we managed to make love. For the next four months I felt like a schoolgirl. I was hung up on him.

When my husband eventually tried to make a move toward me, I almost threw up. I wouldn't let him touch me. As far as I was concerned, everything was finished between us. I could not make love to two men at the same time. I started losing weight and crying and being up all night long. All I could think about was being with this man who was so good and here I was stuck in the house with a man who was so horrible. I lost fifteen pounds. I looked like a skeleton and my husband didn't even notice.

Finally, I asked for a separation. My husband said, "I didn't even know you were unhappy." He just thought I was going through a screwy period. I came close to a breakdown. My heart was fluttering and I had to get pills from the doctor. I couldn't breathe and I thought I was going to die. My husband wouldn't agree to a separation.

My lover was getting serious and started talking about getting married. I had no desire to get married. I wasn't even unmarried. We drifted apart. I was glad when the affair ended. I didn't have to sneak around any more.

Eventually my husband said he would give me a divorce, but he wouldn't leave the house until it was final. He said if he didn't need sex then neither did I, and if he ever caught me with another man, he'd take the children away from me so fast it would make my head spin. For a year and a half I couldn't sleep with anyone else, go out with anyone else, or even have lunch with anyone else.

During this period I got myself into a terrible experience.

I was flying home from picking up my son when I decided to stop in Chicago to see a football game. I was still friendly with my former lover, and his football team was playing. I wanted to see the game. I ended up in the same hotel as the football team. When I phoned my husband, he was angry and upset that I had stayed over.

The next morning my son went downstairs and came racing back up and said, "Guess what? Dad's downstairs!"

I said, "You're kidding!" I was so terrified and upset that I sent my son down to talk to him and tell him not to come up. I left my room and went down the hallway where I ran into a couple of football players and gals sipping champagne before the game. They offered me some champagne and I started talking to two of the fellows and told them why I was standing there. They had to go downstairs and eat their pre-game lunch. Then one fellow said he had a color television in his room and I could stay there and hide if I didn't want my husband to find me. I decided to do that and both fellows went downstairs. Later one of the men came back, closed the door, and came over and picked me up. He was an enormous black fellow. I asked what he was doing.

He said, "I'm going to kiss you."

I asked why and he answered, "Because I like you."

He told me he was going to make love to me, and I told him he wasn't. I was still terrified that if anyone found out, I'd lose the kids. He took my clothes off and forced me down on the bed.

I kept protesting and asking him not to do it. I really didn't want him to.

Just as he was finishing, his roommate came in. I stormed into the bathroom, yelling how disgusted I was with the one who had screwed me. I still wasn't afraid. Then the other one came into the bathroom naked. I climbed up on the sink to get away from him. He was really ready to go. I was fighting him until I realized all the wiggling going on must be terribly exciting to this man. I quit wiggling and he picked me up and carried me into the bedroom. The other guy was just standing there. I looked up at him from the bed and yelled, "If you're not going to stop this, then the least you could do is not watch." The second guy finished when the telephone rang. It was his wife. He put his hand over my mouth because I threatened to scream.

The guy put his wife on hold and the two of them went flying around the room trying to find my clothes, so I could put them on.

I got dressed and I said to the guys, "You're really creeps. You're nothing but animals!" As I was walking out the door, another fellow walked in and one of them said to him, "Too late, you missed the boat."

I went back to my room. My husband didn't come up. I later wrote them a letter telling them what they had done was ugly. I also told them they were rotten lovers. I wrote, "You don't have the faintest clue how to treat a woman. You don't grab her and rip her clothes off and treat her like that!"

Later, they called me up and apologized. They said they hoped they hadn't hurt me physically. They thought my being in their room was an absolute open invitation. I told them it wasn't. They asked me if we could be friends and they offered me box seats for the next game.

Looking back on that experience, I can honestly say I wasn't the least bit afraid. What did scare me was that they were so strong; there was nothing I could have done. If someone said to me, "You could have stopped them!" it wouldn't be true. All they had to do was hold me with one arm.

Shortly after that, I was divorced. My affairs since then have been long-term and satisfying. I dated a European man for five years. I love European men and men who have emigrated from other countries. They are willing to try new things and go out on a limb. It doesn't matter if they have to starve to death for a year, they know they'll eventually make it. The European man taught me many things, including that life without problems isn't life. I now regard problems as a challenge, something to figure out.

My latest boyfriend is the first man I ever went after. He's fifty and he didn't realize there was so much of life left. When I met him he said, "I'm an old man." I said, "No, you're not!" I've been training him for two years. If you find a man with the basic qualities, you can train him. It's just difficult to find any man older than forty who's still interesting, sexually attractive, and interested in life. Men are thirty-nine one day and eighty the next.

Men find me attractive and fun because I don't talk about marriage. I've never thought about marrying again. I can't imagine liking someone for the rest of my life.

I never mess around on the first date because I don't know if I'm going to like the man the second time I see him. He has to have some reason to come back. I have a friend who hasn't had a relationship for years because, after twenty minutes, she lets a man know she wants to go to bed with him. I tell her that you have to be good to him, but say at the end of the evening, "I think you're really nice, and maybe some-day I'll go to bed with you, but tonight isn't the time."

I'm glad I saw choices and took them. Not seeing choices means you're in a rut. Sometimes I think about all the things I don't know and have to learn and I'm afraid I won't have the time to learn. So I keep planning trips, mastering new subjects, and meeting new people. I thoroughly enjoy myself.

5 Jane, Laura, and Francine

Jane

Jane is twenty-six with short red hair, freckles, and large blue eyes. She was married at twenty, separated at twenty-three. Her background is rural middle-class.

I come from a small town and getting married in a small town is a big social affair. I married at twenty because it was what everybody did. Everyone thought my husband and I were the perfect couple. After a year we moved to Seattle, where there was a career opportunity for my husband. As it turned out, my husband lacked ambition. He didn't want any change in life and found a job similar to the one he had back home. At night all he wanted to do was sit at home and watch TV.

My first extramarital affair was a one-night stand. It happened after an office party, with my boss. It was an encounter caused by sheer proximity. The situation was there, my boss was there, and we were both drunk and horny.

It was fun, but the next day I felt badly, and I didn't want it to happen again. I felt guilty because I thought it was morally wrong. What bothered me was the fact I'd actually slept with someone other than my husband. My marriage vows haunted me during that night and through my subsequent affairs. I was conscious of the fact that I was married the entire time, so mentally I wasn't totally there during the sexual experience. Although I had a good time, I was really reserved. But after a number of months and a number of men, the feeling of guilt lessened and I looked forward to extramarital sex as a release.

For the last six months of my marriage all I could think about was getting out, splitting up, but I couldn't make a move. I continued to go out and go to bed with different men. Usually, I was drunk when I picked them up in a bar. The first month I must have had different men three times a week. I was really insane. I just said to hell with it. After about a month my conscience started to bother me, although this wild, drunken phase lasted about three more months.

After that, I began to pick up men I could relate to; I began being choosy. At the same time I would become infatuated very quickly with these men, but they were all involved with someone else so the affairs ended up being short-term. I hated the words, "I'll call you." I knew that meant a man didn't want me to phone him. Chances were he wouldn't phone. I hated being rejected.

Most of the affairs were mediocre. They just satisfied the physical and emotional need of the moment. I realize I was testing myself, exploring what I was capable of. I was finding myself.

When I was infatuated with someone I was always worried about what he was up to, and what he was doing behind my back. I didn't trust people. All along I was really after more than a one-night stand. If I'd had too much to drink and ended up with someone I didn't care about then I never wanted to see him again. When I became infatuated I was the first one to want total commitment.

Most of that entire period I would like to forget. I went to bed with men without thinking. If I'd stopped and thought about it, I would have bolted. I didn't make any decisions.

I didn't like myself very much during that period. I didn't feel true to myself—or I didn't feel like it was really me doing it. I was terrified of picking up some venereal disease. I never remained friends with any of these men, nor did I want to see any of them again. I just wanted to forget the whole business. I felt ashamed of myself.

Sexually, the affairs were exciting because I was experimenting. Sex at home was routine. My husband was as boring in bed as he was out of bed. I also had been a very passive lover and very reserved. I let the man orchestrate everything. After my extramarital experiences, I became more aggressive and more of an initiator.

I did have two long-term affairs. Each lasted close to a year. One was with a fellow who flew in on business occasionally. I was attached to him for many reasons. We were sexually compatible—he was quite experimental in bed. I felt much freer and less inhibited with this man because he was from out of town. Since I knew he couldn't see me all the time, I didn't worry or feel rejected. Sometimes I would see him twice a month and other times I wouldn't see him for two months.

I liked him as a person. He had a strange sense of humor. It was difficult sometimes to tell when he was joking and when he was serious. But I loved his craziness. There was no sanity to our affair. He would call me at three in the morning and say he was staying at a hotel in town and he wanted me to come over. I'd go over and we'd have a great time, and then say good-bye in the morning. It was my best affair because he was fun, a good friend, and good in bed. There was potential in this relationship; it could have turned into a deeper liaison.

My second long-term affair lasted about eight months. It was with a fellow worker. I saw him about twice a week, but the affair was far too casual for me. There was never anything definite planned. He would just call up and we would get together. I was looking for someone who would be a companion. I wanted some security; the lack of security used to upset me easily. I used to worry whether I'd see these men again even though sometimes I didn't want to.

My husband never said a word about my drinking or my late hours. We continued to have a physical relationship as if nothing had happened, although I fantasized it was someone else I was making love to. I think I was running around to try to bring the conflict in my marriage to a head. I was hoping to force my husband's hand so he would take the responsibility of a decision.

I finally did tell my husband I didn't want to live with him anymore. By that time I felt close to a nervous breakdown. I was drinking too much and it was interfering with my work. I was operating on nervous energy and I had lost almost thirty pounds.

When I finally told him he was crushed, but I felt relieved. He never had affairs; it wouldn't even occur to him.

I moved in with a girl friend, and although I still operated on nervous energy, I was far more choosy about the men in my life. I felt lucky that I hadn't picked up a disease. I spent time doing quiet things like listening to music.

Several months later I met Dale. I was attracted by his appearance. He was a huge baseball player. I met him in a bar and the first time we talked we ended up in an argument about working women. I hated him. The second time we were together it was set up by a friend—Dale needed a date for a dance. He was quieter that night. He was honest, settled, older, and less of a bullshitter than the other men I knew. He ended up crashing at my place that night, though nothing happened. We each regarded the other as a challenge. He said I was a difficult person. After that we kept running into each other at the bar where I hung out. One night we got to talking more deeply and I decided to give him a chance. He didn't seem like the typical guy looking for a screw; he seemed to have respect for me as a person and he wasn't demanding. For the next six months we just had a good time. It was light and fun. There was no emotional security for those months.

He had just left his wife and children, and he still had a strong attachment to them.

Then we reached an intermediate stage, although I still knew it could be good-bye Charlie. But by this time I realized he cared although he couldn't show it. I was frustrated for most of the relationship. It was a rocky road and at many points along the way I felt like checking out. Yet intuition told me I was eventually going to get this guy. Still, I wanted some security. I wanted something calm and I wanted to be settled. During this stage we both drank far too much. Life became more settled when his kids got to know and accept me as part of his life.

Eventually we moved in together. I like our relationship for many reasons. Dale is fun and ambitious. He takes care of the financial responsibilities. I feel very secure, which is a feeling I need.

Our relationship is excellent sexually. Sex is impromptu. We can be watching TV and get the urge. He's reserved in some ways, but not in others. He's reserved about what room we're in, but not about what we do. We feel comfortable with each other, and everything is acceptable as long as we're in the bedroom. We have a real closeness in bed, which comes from being deeply in love. We are also not afraid to communicate with one another. I've become more of an initiator and innovator, and I like it. Dale is a very private person and he doesn't like to be mauled in public. He believes that what goes on between us should be kept between us.

I would never dream of having affairs now. I think it would destroy our relationship if I did have one. In fact, people think I'm crazy because I don't go out when he's tied down with the kids. When I've tried going out without him, I haven't enjoyed myself. I guess I still worry that something is going to go wrong again. It's that old insecurity I have to conquer.

Laura

Laura is forty-eight, a brunet with blue-green eyes. She is good-looking and articulate. She has a Ph.D. from the University of California. She is divorced, has two children, and supports herself as a journalist. Her background is upper-middle-class.

I had no affairs before I was married, but I had them during both of my marriages. None of the men I've had affairs with has been married. I think that's an abiding rule with me. I've never been mixed up with a married man. It's bad enough if one of you is married. If both of you are married, it's really a problem.

I married the first time because I grew up in an era when you had to have a husband. You could have a job, too, but you had to have a husband and children. Those were the years that gave birth to the supermoms. I conformed by marrying and getting a job. In my first marriage I had no children.

About five years after we were married my husband, James, was finishing his residency and staying at the hospital. I was teaching. Our paths hardly crossed; it was the ultimate in growing apart. Doctors should be like priests; they should be celibate, and none of them should get married.

During this period, I had an affair. Actually, I had two affairs, although not at the same time. The first was with an Armenian student who had beautiful dark eyes and who was very well-read. His knowledge appealed to me; I was bored with talking about people's insides.

Later, I met a writer with whom I eventually went west. Just before my husband finished his residency we decided to split up. I went west with the writer and we were together for several years. During the latter part of this period there were two other men as well. One was a painter with an international reputation, the other another writer. This was a free period in my life and I was more interested in my career than in seeking a permanent relationship with a man.

I met my second husband, Jeffery, while teaching and writing on the coast. Jeffery is the most intelligent man I have ever known. We moved in together, eventually married, and had children. I was twenty-nine at the time.

I went through a serious metamorphosis at thirty-nine. I can't explain this metamorphosis without explaining something about my background.

I've wanted different things at different times in my life. At thirty-nine I went through the craziest of all my phases. I ran off and had an affair with a younger man. Then I woke up one morning and thought, "My God, I'm going to be forty soon and I haven't done anything!" That was the beginning of the end of my marriage. Jeff didn't object to my going back to work, but he wanted me to take a secure job instead of pursuing a high-risk career in the creative arts.

Jeff was not supportive then—though he is now. The younger man was supportive; he urged me to take risks. It definitely wasn't the affair that ended my marriage: it was my career. Jeff is liberal about affairs. He knew about my affairs, as did my first husband. I could never be bothered sneaking around. It's not in my nature. Jeff also had an affair and was quite open about it.

Infidelity didn't bother me and I didn't feel guilty. I don't think Jeff felt guilty, either. I couldn't lie about an intense relationship; if you try, you just go from one bad situation to another. It's sad when women have to sneak around. However, there's an old saying that a woman won't give up one man until she finds another. With most women this is true.

My second marriage lasted for thirteen years and we're still very close. We share parenting and we enjoy talking.

Nobody can make you happy but yourself; nobody can make you miserable except yourself. At the same time, every woman needs renewal in her physical life, a reaffirmation that she is a woman. This is where affairs and sexual encounters come in. I'm not talking about a long-lasting relationship. If you have a long-lasting relationship, you have renewal in the beginning, then you develop friendship and sharing. I've been lucky because I've had, with rare exception, long relationships with all the men I've known.

No woman ever gets over the need to have men come on to her. It's a thrill to be looked over lustfully. It's a diversion that makes you feel younger, whole, and desirable. It's not a goal in my life, but when it happens every once in a while it's nice. It doesn't have to culminate in sex; it's enough if it culminates in someone asking. A woman can always say no. I suppose every woman likes to tease a bit. And at certain times, every woman seems to need the ego boost of an affair—whether it is just a flirtation, or ends up in bed.

I haven't had too many quick affairs, although I've had a few. Most of mine have been long-term relationships. I've never gone to bed with a man I didn't learn something from. One was a writer, one an artist, one a professor, one a doctor, a few students, a few film producers . . . I like to talk and I want someone who can talk. Generally I look for someone who is a good conversationalist with a good sense of humor. If I had to give you a physical description of any of the men I had affairs with, I'd be hard-pressed, because I don't remember what most of them look like. I've always been attracted more to personalities than bodies.

I had some emotional ties to the writer, but after him there were several shorter sexual encounters. I didn't feel used when the encounters didn't result in long-term relationships. But there was one I regret.

I met a man who was a professor and we went out several times. His wife had just divorced him and he was what I would call an abused husband. He told me he had a very small penis and that his wife had taunted him for seven years. He had had several very hurtful experiences with several women and he was seeing a psychiatrist.

I felt sorry for him and I did go to bed with him. He was

very small, but he made love very tenderly. But I had to end the affair because we shared so few interests and because he was still among what I call the walking wounded. I am very strong and I need to feel a certain equality of emotional strength in men. When I did end it, he thought it was because of his physical size. I was really mad at myself because it was a difficult affair to end. That was my first experience with an emotionally vulnerable male. Most of the men I have encountered have not been in an emotionally vulnerable state, not in the same sense I have been at the time. I am fortunate in that my periods of vulnerability don't last long and that they stem not from failed human relationships, but from outside circumstances.

I have never had an affair with a man I wasn't friends with first. Even in the case of the rare one-night stand, I have known the men well. In the case of the one-night stands, I think we probably both got drunk. It might not have happened otherwise.

I suppose I do take sex very seriously. Like most women, I've had a few experiences where I've felt used, but those were when I was much younger, and I soon learned to look for a relationship that is solid. As you get older, the desire for just a physical relationship starts to subside. After all, when you're younger, the biological urge is much stronger. When you're older, you want something more. You still want your muscle spasms, but you also want affection and a shoulder to lean against. That's a two-way feeling, since your partner may want to lean on your shoulder, too. You want a relationship where you can talk to him and share activities. If you fall down, you want a man to hold out his hand and help you stand up. When you're young, the emphasis is more on the physical aspect.

There's a saying that men give love to get sex and women give sex to get love. I think this is true in a great many cases. I think as one grows older, it becomes less true. I expect a relationship started when both parties are over forty is different. The bloom is off the rose by that time. Maturity comes late in human life, if at all. It seldom happens before thirty. By thirty you begin to realize you want more than sex and more than any ego reward that comes with pure sexual gratification. Maybe it comes when you start watching your own children. To teenagers it is such an important thing to have a boy friend—not a specific boy friend, just a boy friend. Sometimes I feel I'm living in the fifties when I watch young people. Whatever happened to feminism? It's certainly not around with nineteen-year-old women today. They're right back there with the "I-want-a-boy-to-go-with" syndrome. In North America I don't think women work out of it till they're thirty.

At thirty a number of women go through a desire to have children. There's no question that once you have a child, you have a new dimension in your marriage. When they're small they take a lot of time. You can no longer have that close, all-consuming relationship with your husband. It certainly wreaked havoc with my marriage. The physical relationship is part of the glue that binds. It has to be there, as well as the emotional relationship. The physical relationship is not everything, but it is important to marriage. Sex should be there in an open, honest, satisfactory way. What's dangerous and leads to affairs is a very routine physical relationship. When making love has the same importance in your day as watching the evening news or eating dinner, then a person needs the excitement of someone else and starts to look around. It doesn't always lead to marriage breakdown.

I think many people have affairs and then go back to marriage and pick up their physical relationship with one another. Passion can be recaptured, although I don't think an affair is necessarily what causes a couple to recapture it. Married couples are better off going to a hotel, away from their children, now and again. They have to break the routine of their lives to break the routine of their sex life. Sex without emotion can make you feel used. You can feel even more used in a marriage if your sexual services are no more important than your dishwashing services. The thrill of an affair fills a need if your marriage is routine. You can break that by getting into slightly more exotic circumstances. Many people seem to stay married with dead sex lives—I'm not sure how. It's probably easier to stay married than go through the trauma of divorce.

Relationships are different when you're young. Fumbling can be fun. Yet there's something awful in the thought of two young teenagers in the back seat of a car, neither of them having the vaguest idea of what they're doing. One of my children said it all: "Foreplay's more interesting."

When you are older, there are no bad lovers, although you might get one whose physical attributes appeal to you more than another's. For example, I am hung up on broad shoulders. I like to lean on them. I like silence when I'm making love, not non-movement, but silence. I think in order to enjoy sex, your brain has to be engaged and I always fantasize when I'm making love. A running line of chatter interferes with my fantasies. God forbid anything should interfere with my fantasies. A sexual fantasy, mine at least, usually involves the person I'm with . . . it's the locale I fantasize about.

I don't usually sleep with one man and fantasize about another. I think men do it a great deal, far more than women do. I don't think there's anything wrong with it. All the men I've ever known have told me they fantasize about other women. It's similar to always wanting steak when you have lobster and always wanting lobster when you have steak. You don't think about what you have; you think about what you don't have. Of course, if your fantasy is vivid, you have to get your partner to touch you in the right way so that your physical senses are in tune with your fantasy. It's not always easy.

I have a unique relationship with Carl. It is extraordinary and we're very close, although not necessarily sexually. We go on vacations together and I'm far closer to him than I've ever been to anyone. There are times when this relationship is sexual and times when it is not. In that sense, it's on again, off again, but in all other ways, it is completely steady and we have complete trust in one another.

I don't want to get married again. I'm quite happy the way I am. I'm very much in love with my career. I think I'm incapable of the kind of relationship that marriage requires because I'm totally absorbed in my work. It's consuming—emotionally, physically, and mentally.

Francine

Francine is in her late thirties. She is young-looking and extremely attractive. She works at the management level for an international firm, which she travels for extensively. She was married for seven years, to a dentist. She has been separated for a year and has changed both her profession and the city where she lives.

You only get out of life what you put into it. You have to give of yourself. You can't hide love and warmth because those are the emotions that make life worthwhile. It's great to have material possessions and keepsakes you enjoy, but without love material objects are not enough.

Lovemaking is good and emotions are important. There are some people who control their emotions too much. They might as well be amoebas. It's fun forcing people to come out of themselves, yet I've had some horrible experiences rolling those stones, some of which should never be turned. Some people are better off alone, growing moss, because they can't cope with real life and what life has to offer. Sometimes I think it's better to hate than to feel nothing. People who don't love often can't hate, either. They're so neutral and indifferent. The art of love is something you learn and some people seem to be thwarted in their development of love.

Love can never be destructive. It's not really love if it is destructive, but something else under the guise of love. If we hurt when we don't mean to hurt, then it shouldn't be construed as cruel and mean. It should be overlooked, because the intent was not to hurt. People can be hurt because we don't always know what the other person is thinking. We can never crawl inside another person's thoughts, and some people don't express themselves well. If people could just pass on their thoughts to people in a nonverbal way then perhaps we'd get more out of each other.

If you get into a relationship, you can sometimes confuse sexual gratification with love. The early emotions are sometimes similar. If it's only a sexual attraction, when the sex is over, you are often left with emptiness. Love leads to passion and passion leads to sex. Sometimes we skip the first step and get into passion. If it's been a long time since you've had someone be kind and sweet and loving to you and someone comes along and blows on your neck and kisses your fingers, then you feel passionate.

My affair started because of a lack of affection. I was at a tennis-club meeting, and after the meeting I went to a dance at the club. I was having a beer, talking to people and watching the dancers. One fellow danced quite well. I caught his eye because I thought it would be nice to dance with him. His name was Barry. I'd never met him before, but he finally asked me to join him. He was an attractive man and a challenge because he had been dancing with everyone.

I had been married about six years when I met Barry. He was so full of life; you could tell by the way he danced. After we got to chatting, he asked me to go for a coffee. I had to work the next day, so I thought, well, I'll just go for a coffee. But we never got to the coffee shop. I don't remember what we talked about; what I remember was sitting in his car and necking. The experience was just beautiful; the caresses and kisses were so soft, warm, and sensuous. I had to restrain myself or I certainly would have been in bed with him. He was gentle and loving and a person who really liked people. We just snuggled. I felt guilty, even though I realized one of the reasons I did succumb to Barry was because my husband, George, was so unloving and undemonstrative. George was never affectionate enough to suit me. With Barry there was lots of cuddling. He was like a teddy bear. Necking with him was just great. Nothing else happened in the car—except I was wet between the legs with excitement, something that hadn't happened for about a year. The lubrication was unbelievable, but I didn't attack him because I felt guilty that I was attracted to a man other than my husband. I was basically satisfied with my husband, because we shared so many interests.

After I went home, I thought about Barry a lot. He called me a few days later. My husband was away, so I invited him over. We were all over each other at first, in a nice, warm, sweet way. We necked for hours. Then I thought, "What the hell, who am I kidding? This is the way I feel." We made love on the floor because I didn't want the people next door to hear the bed squeak. It was very nice; he had a different style of lovemaking. We were at right angles to one another and my legs were straight up in the air.

Once, after a tennis-club meeting, I went over to his place. I was all dressed up since I had gone to the meeting from work. He had this big long couch and he started making love to me on the couch while I was still dressed. He went under my skirt and touched me in exciting ways. He took down my panties and pantyhose and started licking me all over, and it was especially erotic because I still had my shoes on. My husband likes sucking and licking, too; it was the only way he could make me come.

Barry and I started seeing each other about once a week. We used to phone each other quite often. Once he called me and I was lying in bed and I had an orgasm, without masturbating, while we talked on the phone. All of a sudden, I just came, but that was just once in my life. Barry was a funny guy; he said he had to make love every day or he'd go nuts. He had a girl friend; sometimes he lived with her.

Actually, we had a lot of fun, although I realized it was just a physical relationship. He was reasonably intelligent and was able to carry on a good conversation. After awhile, though,

I realized Barry really didn't have very much to say. He just wasn't mentally stimulating. That's when I started to get bored. There has to be intellectual stimulation. In any case, I didn't see him for awhile.

Then he called me about a year later and invited me to a picnic. I went and had fun, but he tried to make love to me in the park, under a blanket. I just lay with my back to him, but I think he came anyway. I didn't really care.

During the affair, my sex life at home was terrible. I just hated my husband. I was nasty and threw things around. I was unco-operative and unpleasant. If I wanted something done, I'd just say, "Do it!" I'd storm around the house and make noises with pots and pans. I was mad because I felt I was being taken advantage of by my husband. But really, I was upset with myself. Somehow people don't recognize anger in themselves and tend to sublimate it. It comes out as nastiness rather than anger.

George would try hard, by making meals and doing chores. But I still responded angrily. Wasn't that terrible? My lover and I both remarked how his girl friend and my husband kept trying to be good to us, and we both kept getting nastier and more ornery. I think I was too stupid and too giving to know I was being taken advantage of by my husband. When I did realize it, I was filled with hostility.

Sex became perfunctory with my husband. I didn't care if he touched me. I had known the marriage would end even before the affair. I remember one day, not too long before the affair. My husband was sitting on the couch, and I said to him, "I want to talk to you. We have to talk!"

He said, "What about?"

I answered, "I just don't think there's any love here." I remember sitting on the rug, almost banging my fists on the floor, pleading with him and saying, "Don't you see? Either I don't love you, or you don't love me." Mostly, I think I was trying to say, you don't love me. I was the poor puppy no one loved, saying, "Pet me, love me."

My husband kept saying, "I don't know what you're talking about." I wonder, now that I've left him, if he had ever known what I was talking about.

I felt sorry for my husband. We had just bought a resort condominium, and I felt I had to stay with him to benefit from the material pleasures. We still had many other advantages going for us, but my husband was selfish, totally selfish. Yet the affair made me realize I wasn't going to meet someone who has everything to offer. I thought I could get along with a guy who was selfish because we had all the material distractions. As long as I played the role, we were hunky-dory, but as soon as I didn't, it all collapsed. I just thought I'd grin and bear it. Then his ten-year-old son from his first marriage came to live with us, and a bad situation became worse. I couldn't cope with my job plus two kids at home, my husband being one of them. I had to handle my husband with gloves. I had to manipulate him because that's what he wanted. I had to set the stage and make sure everything was suitable for the play our marriage had become.

I finally left and took a job in Atlanta. It was a job my husband had convinced me I could never do. He enjoyed eroding my confidence.

I have no regrets about leaving George, other than not doing it sooner. I guess I was grasping at straws for a long time. There's a lot of security in a marriage, especially one you have been in for years. You're not cognizant of what's happening. You're totally submerged in the marriage, because it is part of your lifestyle. You think, isn't this normal? You lose sight of what you're really after. You get involved. For instance, my husband and I shared a lot of activities. Perhaps we hid behind those friends and activities for too long. We didn't even notice anything was wrong. He had the perfect robot. She walked, talked, and screwed. He could have had a blow-up doll and I could have disappeared; he would have been just as happy. I think I'd feel sorry for anyone he had now.

After I left my husband, he came to see me and offered me everything—children, security, everything that money could buy. He said he felt he loved me, and he could give me something. It was just awful, woeful and so sad that he would do something like that. He didn't understand that a dishwasher and a maid weren't what I needed. I was perfectly capable of running a household with one hand tied behind my back. He didn't understand that I was too tired to placate someone who didn't appreciate me as a person. My husband was spoiled and almost incapable of love. Even his son used to try to get George to show him some affection.

The day my husband came to see me, he had been reading an article about marriages and why they break up. George realized what he had to hear from me was that I didn't love him any more. It was a little like death. He had to recognize the death of the relationship. I said to him, "I don't love you any more." I don't know if it was true, but I said it anyway. He needed to hear it. If you keep hoping, then you don't move on to anything else. You can go forward to a new relationship if you have no hope the old one will survive.

6 Mary Lynn, Sharon, and Marie

Mary Lynn

Mary Lynn is thirty-four. She is a librarian and an identical twin. She comes from an upper-middle-class background.

It's still rather hard for me to talk about my affair with Rory. I still feel guilty about it.

Perhaps if I told you about me, about my childhood, it would help put things in perspective. I'm a twin and somehow I think that played a role, though I'm not sure how. My sister and I are identical twins and while we look different from each other now, we resembled each other very closely when we were young. My mother always dressed us alike and one of us couldn't do anything at all unless the other did it, too. I never really felt like a person in my own right. Heavens! Even my sister's name is similar to mine. She's Sue Lynn and I'm Mary Lynn.

Sue Lynn and I were very close. We went to university together and we roomed together in the same sorority house. We were married on the same day in a double ceremony.

Our choice of men, though, wasn't the same. Sue Lynn married a real bastard, at least I think he's a bastard. Oh, he takes care of Sue Lynn materially, but he's never there for her. He owns his own advertising agency, and he's always traveling. I really think he's unfaithful to her and that has frightened me quite a bit. I guess I can't afford to throw stones, at least not anymore, but I wish Jack was better to her.

Maybe that's why I still feel guilty about Rory and me. I guess I feel Sue Lynn and my husband, Howard, have something in common. I feel sorry for both of them sitting at home while Jack and I have our flings.

I'm not sure what made me do it. I've thought and thought about it. The only thing I can come up with is that Howard never takes chances. "No-risk Howard"—that's what I call him. Howard is quiet, conservative, safe and non-threatening—but no fun. Just like my job. Howard doesn't complement the rest of my life, my work that is. You can't really have a safe job, go home to a safe house, on a safe street, and not go crazy. That is unless you're dead, and I'm not. Howard couldn't even bother to set up his own law practice. He wanted set vacations and a pension instead. Other attorneys that went on their own are now making tons of money. They travel around the world and I'd like to do that, too. The money we make is fine, but we both have to keep working to keep it coming in. A little risk from Howard would have made life more exciting for both of us.

I should take some chances myself. I know that. I think about that often. The only chance I really took was my affair with Rory and I was so mad at my life that I was anybody's game. I just had to show myself I could take a chance. The affair was impulsive and dangerous. It could have easily ruined my life.

Anyway, that was the mental shape I was in when I first laid eyes on Rory. He's younger than I am, about nine years younger. I met him on a faculty-graduate-student library committee. We met three times a month for a year for committee meetings and I always noticed he was smiling at me. He was playing with me mentally and sexually. I like that.

I like to see a man undress me with his eyes, and I like to see a funny twisted smile on a man's face when a really dirty thought crosses his mind.

So I guess I started playing games with him. For the whole first year we just developed the sexual game. It's fun when you're sitting there with all these staid academics who are being so pompous. And Rory and I were playing at being so sexy and funny. The meetings were bearable because of Rory. I never missed one.

I guess I finally realized I was on the brink of an affair when I started thinking about Rory whenever Howard made love to me. Howard isn't a bad lover. He knows my body well. He touches me in all the right places and he's slow enough and waits for me to come. But I just kept thinking about Rory. Rory would do something insane, something really nuts. Rory would crush me. He'd turn me over and enter me from behind. He'd be gutsy and different. Well, I was always excited for Howard when I thought of Rory. But afterwards I started to resent Howard and think, "You stupid fool. How insensitive can you be? I want to fuck Rory and you don't even know it." I began to resent Howard for not being Rory. Boy, was I a mess.

The whole experience was making me feel guilty. I didn't want to sleep with my own husband any more. Howard kept saying, "How come, when it was so good there for a while?" I didn't have any answers at first and then I started to use the excuse of bleeding mid-month and having to see a gynecologist to straighten out my problems.

Finally Rory asked me out for coffee. I guess he had waited so long because the game we had was such fun. I knew something was going to happen that night. I phoned Howard and told him I had to stay in the city because I couldn't get the car started and because of the snow. I said I'd try to get home but I wasn't sure when. Howard suggested it was safer for me to stay at a hotel. That gave me all the time I needed with Rory. I felt guilty, but relieved at the same time.

Rory took me to his place for coffee. He lived in an attic

on the top floor of an old Victorian house near the university. He only had one small room with a hot plate and a fridge and this enormous round bed, which dominated the entire room. Incense was burning. Rory's world was as far from Howard's as I could get.

Rory fixed us some espresso and brought out a bottle of anisette. He turned on some music, sat down, smiled at me, and asked me if I wanted to fuck. He was that direct. I guess my face went red and I mumbled something idiotic about not wanting to get a venereal disease. Rory just laughed and grabbed my breast and said, "You gotta take some chances."

Those were the perfect words for my ears, and that was how it started. Rory was the first man whose pants I unzipped. It was a real turn-on for me. Being aggressive sexually was fun: I felt more potent than I ever felt in my whole life.

That was the first time I ever fucked the night away. For three hours we just kept going. We'd do it one way and then another and another and another. After a while I started to get sore and laughed about having to wear a bandage home to Howard.

Rory taught me much about experimenting and trying new things. I found out about myself sexually. I didn't know I had so many nerve endings. It's exciting to know how far your body can go and how much enjoyment your body can handle. Rory learned a lot from me, too. So that was satisfying. He really loved my body in a unique way and I guess that's what I wanted out of the whole affair. A new appreciation of myself and my body.

Rory and I broke up after a year and a half. It was fun while it lasted. He transferred to another university when he became a teaching assistant in philosophy. I'll always remember Rory as being one of the better things that happened in my life. We see each other at conferences now and again, but it will never be the same.

I still can't sleep with my husband. I'm now realizing that I can't stand not taking risks. I can't stand living the same life year after year. I believe Rory taught me how to grow and learn as a person. Now I have to deal with Howard. It will take me a while to decide whether to divorce him.

I still can't get myself to tell my sister about my affair with Rory. I feel it's something private, all mine, that I have to remember.

Sharon

Sharon is forty and has a career with the government. She lives in Ottawa and commutes from her suburban home in Kanata. She is a tall, willowy woman with skin like a china doll. Sharon is married; her husband is president of his own firm. They have no children.

I don't like to play it safe with life. I always fight like hell not to get in a rut. Affairs are my way of combating boredom. They're exciting and I feel as if I'm living dangerously. I like to feel I'm gambling with my life. Even the fear that I might screw up my marriage is exciting. During my affairs I feel more alive in every way; I feel frivolous, which is marvelous. Affairs are exhilarating. They take you away from the boring nine-to-five pace of life. It's exciting and enlivening for me to know someone else finds me fascinating. I also believe people are at their healthiest mentally and physically when they are free and independent. I think marriage—being tied to one person—makes people insecure and clinging.

I also want to have my cake and eat it, too. Being married and having affairs means no man can have one-hundred-percent control over you. That kind of independence is extremely attractive to males; they keep coming back to a woman like that. When you are free and secure within yourself and able to be happy on your own, it is irresistible to men. That kind of attitude hooks them.

When you're married and having affairs, your husband provides security. The affair is fantastic when it is happening, but you know there is always someone to run back to if anything goes wrong. It's the same thing as when you are younger and have to have a boy friend. Women always like to have someone around for special occasions like New Year's Eve. With marriage there is still that measure of security.

I think I'm afraid of ending up alone one day. If I play goody-two-shoes while my husband has been having affairs all along, I'm going to feel left out, and I think I'll be sorry if I let all the opportunities for affairs go by. I'm proud—I don't want people to think of me as a poor soul. I want to be able to say I've had affairs, too. Anyway, no one's perfect, and I don't want to be perfect. That's boring and dull.

I think affairs have helped my marriage, especially my sex life. When you get into the habit of having sex you want more sex. And when you're eager, that's a turn-on for your husband. I never fantasize about these other men when I'm having sex with my husband. I've tried, but I can't.

Sex is important in my affairs, but there must be more. The most important aspect is communication. I love mental stimulation. I enjoy being with someone I feel comfortable with, I can laugh easily with, and can talk to about many subjects. My first affair, which started about a year after I was married, was this kind of a friendship. I think a good friendship is basic and is a beautiful thing.

My second affair was the best. It started several years after I was married and continued while I was separated, although I didn't leave my marriage for Paul, my lover. This second affair had a kind of sexual chemistry and magnetism that was wonderful and overwhelming. There was more sex than talking with Paul because we weren't compatible on all levels. Paul reminded me of the first lover I had had, when I was twenty-two. With Paul it was magic, and I fantasized that I had my first lover all over again.

I was very much in love with Paul. I felt terribly close and intimate in my relationship with him. He was a genuine person and I knew he thought highly of me. For sex to be good, I have to respect the man, and I have to know he respects me. I knew when I was not out of sight, I was not out of mind, because Paul always did thoughtful little things for me.

But the affair and my love for him scared me. I was afraid the same thing that happened with my first lover would happen in my affair with Paul. With my first lover I felt I was almost destroyed by loving too much. I was so caught up in love, I wanted him night and day, I couldn't think about anything else. I could make love to my pillow thinking about him. That kind of sexual attraction and love is obsessive and deadly. I was afraid to be so much in love; I couldn't think and I couldn't be objective. I didn't like it when I began to feel my happiness depended completely on him.

After several months, and especially when I was separated, I felt so good when I knew Paul and I were going to be together on the weekend that all week I'd have a high energy level. I'd race through my work. I was on top of the world, lively and excited. But when something went wrong and our plans fell through, I'd get depressed and introverted and spend hours staring at the ceiling. I just hated someone having that control over my life and my emotions. I was always happiest when I was independent. I was afraid of losing control over myself. I was afraid of that kind of love. I don't plan to have anyone dominate my life to that extent again. I can't deal with it, when everything I do in life has meaning only because that person is involved in it, and doesn't have any meaning when that person is not around. I eventually had to choose between my husband and Paul. Paul became highly possessive and forced me to make a decision. I chose my husband because I care about him, but I can still be independent and do my own thing.

I don't trust love and I don't think about love anymore. I'd much rather have someone like me and respect me than love me. Love can become too emotional and too up-and-down. I don't want to base anything on love, because I don't feel safe with love. I really don't like someone who shows too much emotion. I don't trust it.

I want my lovers and my husband to respect me for my intelligence and for the job I do. I could never stand anyone who appeared to be dying for me. Someone who comes on too strong is a bore. I admire someone who has backbone, who has his own ideas, who is not a pushover. It's weird how you really want a man to want you, and yet you also want him to be independent and keep his elusive quality. I suppose a man is more of a challenge if he can take me or leave me.

I don't want someone who makes a fool out of me. I want someone who treats me as a person. I also want discretion. I respect a lover who doesn't kiss and tell. I don't want to give any of the people around me something to amuse themselves with. I really dislike gossip and people who gossip. Discretion and respect are the mark of a man. I don't like men who act like little boys.

My affairs have been mostly with single men, but I feel married men are safer, since they don't or can't talk about their affairs. And the chances of picking up a social disease may be less. With married men I prefer the one-night stand. I don't want a relationship that's going to continue. I don't let any of the men who interest me know I desire them because I don't want anything more than a few nights. Men tend to cling more than women do, and I don't want anyone who is going to fall in love with me.

Sex has always died first in my affairs, but we were always good friends later. Sexually, I'm still a rather closed person. I don't enjoy a lot of changes. I still feel bashful about some things. I still have certain hang-ups. I don't want to be asked to do something I consider outrageous; I've never really felt free enough with someone to abandon myself. I actually feel most free with my husband. I know I can suggest things, and I do like a lot of foreplay. I like orgasm, too, but I enjoy all the preliminaries because they add to the intensity.

I don't have affairs now, although I'd still like to. I really could have gone on and on, but I feel guilty now. I told my husband about the affairs before anyone else could tell him. Now I can't get away with extramarital affairs because he doesn't trust me. My husband didn't want to talk about my affairs, and he didn't ask any questions. I think he probably has one-night stands, but I don't want to know about them. My husband and I do have strong ties and we motivate one another. A boring person would just kill me. Still, you're not human if you're not looking.

Marie

Marie is a thirty-five-year-old New Yorker from a working-class background. She now lives in Canada. She is married and has a successful and creative career. She works with her husband. Marie is tall, blond, and has large hazel eyes.

Being close to people is important to me: I like to watch people think. I like to observe their minds in motion and I love making them laugh and watching them enjoy themselves. For me, men are easier to know than women, and there's nothing closer than the intimacy of sex. You get to know a man and how he feels; you get to know his skin and his scent. It's understanding men that I like; that's what I aim for. I have had many affairs, and each has brought me something interesting. My knowledge of men has eliminated any need for me to be a feminist in the true sense; by that I mean I know that some men are stupid and vacuous while others are truly intelligent and dynamic. Knowing men has given me perspective. I know men as human beings; they're no different from women and they don't have any special keys to the kingdom.

Having affairs and seeing men intimately has given me the

satisfaction and knowledge that I married the right guy. I'll never have to wonder if I missed anything because I've seen it all. I know for sure that I got the best, the very best, and I'm proud of my husband. There're no doubts in my mind and that has given me a freedom that I find precious.

The man I married was one of my affairs when I was living with Herb. Herb and I lived together for four years and were essentially married. I wouldn't commit myself on paper until I knew a marriage would work. I hate the law and didn't want to have to undo any damage a marriage license would cause both of us. I'd seen too many divorces, and I knew I didn't want to go through all the ugliness and sense of failure that a legal divorce entails—so I avoided the paperwork. Herb and I were happy together; we didn't have much in the way of material things, but we laughed and had a good time. The only problem was that Herb knew less about everything than I did and that troubled me. As a child I always dreamed of marrying a really bright man. Herb was physically attractive and very masculine and I was proud of him, but his lack of knowledge led me to be a person I didn't want to be; I was bored and frustrated intellectually. Herb was also in a rut. He was a furniture mover, and such a lowly job for someone with a college education just didn't sit well with me. He was career-ineffectual: nothing worked. And he was afraid of growing and learning. When someone is stuck in time and not moving forward, you look into an empty, unchanging future and your hopes dwindle. Toward the end, the relationship just fizzled out. I put Herb on automatic—emotionally, I just wasn't there anymore. I came to think of him in the way I thought of my girl friends; someone to be with, someone to have a good time with. Nothing more.

My own career was running into trouble at the time and that hurt and confused me. One of my great escapes from all ills is to flop into a man's arms. Sex gives me reassurance. It takes me out of myself and gives me a real change. Men also make life more glamorous for me. New men feel a fantastic need to treat you beautifully and impress you, and I need that feeling of power. Most of my life at the time was pretty dull and I certainly couldn't afford any of the finer clubs in New York on my salary. I wasn't above picking men up and allowing them to show me a good time. I felt— I still feel—that youth is fleeting. Grab the good times while you can. I like having a hell of a good time. To that end I developed a good system of sitting in bars and cafes waiting to be picked up. I have a well-developed sense of survival. I have street smarts from growing up in New York City and can pick up the right men. By "right" men, I mean the sane and the interesting ones. Many have money, and that makes it even better. Wealth, powerful careers, and an inside knowledge of other classes and lives intrigues me. Many of the men I picked up were from foreign countries: South Africa, Peru, Denmark, Britain, and from other states in America. Texas oil men, international attorneys, doctors, and psychiatrists are just a few of the occupations I encountered in my travels. Many of the men were staying at grand New York hotels, and breakfast the morning after was always exquisite. The sex was good, too. Many of these men were well-educated and sensitive to a woman's needs. Their careers were developed, their lives stimulating and interesting, and they had no need to do anything but enjoy a night on the town in New York and have some quiet sex.

For example, I had an affair with Ben, who was an accountant for a huge corporation with offices in Peru, the States, France, and other countries of the world. He was a walking monopoly; the only man in the world with his specific knowledge. We saw each other every three months or so, and it was fun. We'd meet at the Waldorf and he'd take me shopping and buy me dresses and shoes and pay to have my hair done and then we'd go out. We would start with dinner at a four-star restaurant; then we'd have cocktails in a quiet piano bar, and go back to the hotel. The sex was loving and caring. He really liked me, and I liked him. It was good in a sweet, sensitive way and I liked that. I'm not a hellfire in bed and I appreciate and enjoy sweetness and cuddling more than the wildly erotic. During my relationship with Ben, I learned a great deal about the world and got a taste of what it was like to have money.

I came from a working-class family, but my affairs brought me up to a higher level of existence. Without these affairs I would never have known how the better half lived; I would have had no idea of splendor or elegance. I'm not stupid, and the affairs led to a complete change in my expectations. I began to expect a lot from my long-term relationships. I began to ask for the best. When you ask, you receive, and now both my husband and I ask a lot from life and we're both willing to work for it.

My affair with Gary started at a convention in California. He was from Canada, a buyer for a chain of stores. We were in the same industry and had a lot in common. I hated him when we first met; he made fun of my promotional broadcast. He stood there and laughed and cracked jokes throughout my presentation, and I wanted someone to shut him up he was so obnoxious. Later that day at a cocktail party, this idiot, Gary, found me with a group of salesmen he couldn't stand, so he butted in and grabbed me away. I really didn't care for those salesmen anyway, so I started to talk with him. Then things started happening; he was one of the most powerful buyers at the convention and so the president of my firm asked us both to have dinner with him. What could I say? I had to go, and I had to dine with this obnoxious buyer and the people from his company. For some strange reason we got along, and after dinner we went for some drinks alone. We got along better and better and landed up in bed together. I didn't exactly like the idea of sleeping with one of the buyers from a top account, but I said, "What the hell." Gary was nice enough, and he told me exactly why he laughed at my presentation—and he apologized. We got on well, the sex was good, and I felt good. He left for Atlanta the next day for another business meeting and I never expected to see him again. When I returned home to Herb, I didn't mention it. I figured Herb would never know.

Then Gary started taking extra business trips to New York so he could see me. Herb began to realize that our relationship was finished. He decided to move out, and I had to move because I couldn't afford the rent by myself. I moved into a cheap apartment down the street. Gary came often and I traveled to Toronto, where Gary lived, for weekends every once in a while. Six months later Gary asked me to move to Toronto. Since my job didn't feel good or secure anymore, I just chucked everything and moved. It happened fast. I still can't believe everything just fell into place.

Herb left me without a whimper, even though I knew he cared deeply about me, and I thought I loved him. Everything happened as if it was fated. Never in my wildest imagination did I think about marrying Gary or living with him until he asked me to move to Toronto. If I had been doing well at my job it might never have happened. I grew to love Gary in time. He's a hard one to get to know, but once you know him you really can't help but love him. Gary has always been good to me and our love grows with time. Each year is better than the one before.

Now I'm the seasoned veteran of many affairs while my friends are getting divorced and going through the process of getting to know men all over again. They married early, before they knew what they were doing. Sometimes I'd like to have an affair now, but I have too much to lose. Gary is too perfect for me—I can't take the chance.

7 Annie, Marsha, and Loretta

Annie

Annie is forty. She has been married for seventeen years and as a housewife has been responsible for rearing two children. She is a high-school graduate and comes from a middle-class family.

My affair with Arthur was not a conscious, well-thought-out action. It was not brought about by vengeance or any sort of dislike for my husband: I love Harold dearly. It came about as a result of frustration, partially sexual and partially because my role as a mother was becoming less demanding, and I was at a loss to fill up spare time. We were secure with Harold's salary. But security or not, we had a problem. Harold is a stockbroker and his desire to make love to me seemed to rise and fall with the market. Later his heavy drinking made unbearable a relationship that was once bearable. Too many nights Harold would fall asleep in the middle of our lovemaking. He would say something like, "Guess I had one too many last night, right honey?"

This pattern continued despite our efforts to talk over our problems. Harold's stubbornness, male pride, and his explanation—"It will be better next time"—became a regular routine. There would then usually follow the expensive "I-love-you" gifts—a Cartier watch, a new dress, a pair of shoes, exquisite diamond earrings, and other beautiful gifts. Harold has excellent taste, but all these bribes didn't work. They were no substitute for the love and affection that Harold used to give so generously. Have you ever tried to make love to diamond earrings? They are not always a girl's best friend.

I felt terrible, lost, and empty inside. Was it me who caused Harold to drink so much? Was the pressure of his job too much? I'm sure that being responsible for other people's millions of dollars has got to be draining.

Once we tried to go away and capture the past excitement by visiting the honeymoon capital, Niagara Falls. The falls at night are fantastic, those beautiful lights catching the mist and making it sparkle as it rises. Harold can be so romantic when he's away from the phone. We did everything, the moonlit carriage ride, the ballroom dancing, the long walks. I told Harold I wanted to feel that I was important to him and that Dow Jones was secondary. I even asked him if I was still sexually attractive.

We tried to communicate, but he was still very tense. He mentioned something about a big stock deal. I don't know much about his work; my interests are more in the arts, the little theater in town. He claimed he still loved me and still found me attractive. That night he tried to prove it. We changed our room to one that had a queensized waterbed. I thought, this is the wildest! That is, I thought that once I accepted that the mattress wouldn't burst and drown the both of us. We were rolling and playfully wrestling, undressing each other one sock at a time, kissing, pinching, tickling, licking, and giggling like a couple of teenagers. The wave action in those beds is great as long as you don't get motion sickness, and Harold is 180 pounds, with muscular, broad shoulders, a tight hairy bum, long legs, and all his parts were doing their duty. My Harold can be a real hunk. I was going crazy, on the verge of ecstasy, when the bloody phone started ringing. I pleaded with Harold not to answer it. I swear, I think God hired the phone company to do contraceptive work or prevent my pleasure. I could feel Harold leaving me as he reached for the phone. It was a business cronie who was having some trouble with one of the deals they were working on. I tried to get Harold back into bed and in the mood again, but it was no go. We had to leave early in the morning so Harold could look after business. He apologized profusely, and I thought, "This can't go on forever, business will have to settle down eventually." But my patience is limited.

My affair happened by chance a few months later. One of my girl friends, Maggie, got me involved in doing costumes for a spring musical at a local theater. She knew I was good with clothes and that I loved plays. The little theater was great for meeting people; it kept me busy and made me feel useful. I discovered, to my delight, that I had some creative abilities that I never knew about. Working with theater people can be liberating, exciting, and definitely crazy—anything can happen. I sort of knew Arthur casually. He was playing the lead, the pirate king in our musical, *The Pirates of Penzance.* It wasn't until I started fitting him for his costume that I began to feel attracted to him—almost unconsciously. Arthur is twenty-nine, tall, with sandy hair, deep blue eyes, a slender build, and a deep, sexy voice. Arthur wanted to become a professional actor. He had done a little TV work and a couple of ads.

The little theater was paying him a modest salary to be in our musical. I was definitely attracted to those blue eyes and that sexy voice. He was totally different from Harold. He called me ma'am during the first fitting. That really upset me. I stepped back from him, with my pins in hand and said, "Annie's the name. Call me Annie, if you don't want to become a pincushion."

He laughed and agreed to call me Annie. He agreed that I was pretty, and that I had a nice figure, too. What else could he say without risking a pin in the butt? We started talking about the show, his acting career, my costuming, and my children.

On the next fitting I was choosing between tights and baggy pants for his costume. Those tights certainly looked cute. At that moment, while I was literally gawking at his balls, I realized that I was physically attracted to him. I think he knew from the way I was staring. In the end he had to wear the baggy pants. Pity.

He asked me if I was still married, and I said yes, and said things weren't going too well with my husband. I asked him about his status. He said his girl friend left him to be with a TV producer. She had her ambitions, and producers can find parts for aspiring actresses. His personal life wasn't great at that moment, either.

We had coffee after the fitting and I found myself opening up to him, telling him about Harold and my personal frustrations and how I was trying to hold things together, but not quite making it. Arthur listened without passing judgment. He confessed that he found me the most attractive forty-year-old woman he'd ever met and hoped that I would save him a dance at the opening-night party. I felt like a teenager about to embark on her first romance.

Arthur seemed to like me and by now I had decided to let my husband work out his own problems. Around that time Harold and I had a big row over the kids' school reports. Somehow our whole relationship got into the argument. He slapped me for the first time since I've known him and told me I was being childish. That did it. I moved into the spare room and decided to worry about myself and the kids.

The opening-night party was a great success. Arthur and I danced and let loose. Arthur is one great dancer. Talk about being felt up; that guy's hands were all over me in the dark shadows of the dance floor. I was loving it! Any prudishness I had was given up that night.

Finally I said to him, "Do we have to be so public about this? Can't we go someplace?" I was feeling bold. I wanted Arthur to stop drinking before he became useless; I've been through that enough. Phones and alcohol were my worst enemies. Arthur was the perfect gentleman, and questioned me as to how certain I was. I told him that I was game if he was. So we grabbed a bottle of champagne, said our good-byes, and away we went.

Arthur was living in an old one-room apartment with a large brass double bed. We wasted no time. He undressed me by undoing my blouse with his teeth, pulled down my zipper in the same fashion, and nuzzled me. I get excited just thinking about it. Talk about great hands—so sensitive, knowing, and gentle. God, I love youthful exuberance. I hadn't been able to rid myself of so much tension in months. I was beginning to wonder whether I was good in bed any-more since Harold stopped making love with me. It was like being reborn—being with a man who listens, cares about bringing you out of yourself and caring for him in return is beautiful. It's wonderful for however long it lasts, even for one night.

The next day, when you come back to earth again, that's the hard part. You have to ask yourself: What do I really feel for my husband, with whom I've shared so many years, and for the children? Can I run off with this man into the total unknown, and possibly be left behind for some younger and more beautiful actress?

Do I have feelings of guilt? No, not for being with Arthur. Guilt for not getting some help to see if I could be more supportive of Harold? Yes, but I could help him only if he took more interest in me, let me grow into a person with more than a housewife's role. I wanted a role that would give me the feeling of being useful in the community, a recog-nition of other talents that I have.

I do feel guilty about the affair—I felt I was betraying Harold's trust. I haven't told him about it.

Incidently, Arthur left town after finishing the run at our theater and went to join another company. I stayed home. A short while later, Harold collapsed with an ulcer after one of his deals fell through. With my new-found confidence I told him either he must retire and do something more relaxing or I would leave him before I became a widow. Fortunately the doctor was backing me all the way. Still, it was hard to be hitting the man I have loved when he was down. I had to do it because I cared enough about him and our children to force him to see the light. He took my suggestion after a lot of persuading.

Marsha

Marsha is thirty-two years old. She is an interior decorator who runs her own successful business. Middle-class and university-educated, she was recently divorced after being separated for two years from her husband.

I know I need to be loved. Love gives me the reassurance that I'm valuable as a person. If I don't feel loved, I feel tired, depressed, and about a hundred years old. I never thought of myself as someone who needed a lot of attention, but I do need company and verbal reassurance that I'm okay. I think we all tend to take each other for granted once we are married. The relationship is so secure we assume the other person knows our feelings. But love needs nourishment to continue. It needs someone doing special things, little things from the heart, that are unexpected, to let you know someone cares.

I tend to take one day at a time and live it to the fullest. My father died when I was just a child. I realized nothing is permanent and that we are all living on borrowed time. If we all realized that, we could dispense with much of the bullshit so prevalent today. Why are people so afraid to be themselves? Do they imagine people are attracted to them for money or position? Living like this has made me live and love more intensely. I took risks and revealed my feelings because I didn't want to waste time playing games or worrying about the consequences of taking that risk. I feel sorry for people who can't make a move. People like that don't live. You don't live and grow unless you gamble. Mind you, it's always easier when you have nothing to lose.

I've never regretted anything I've done. The worst feelings arose from lost opportunities, whenever I've decided to be sensible rather than take a chance. Gambling is the marvelous feature about life, the force that keeps me going. You never know what's going to happen. I've become hooked on this feeling. Sometimes I like change just for the sake of change. I'm a very restless person; I like to cram as much life into me as I can get. I'm not afraid as long as I don't hurt anyone. Without risks, you never experience the joys and the highlights of life.

Love is one of the highlights of life and one of the emotions I crave. When I love, I feel fantastic, on top of the world, as if every part of my being has come alive. I feel brighter, better, and the best in me comes out like gangbusters. I feel exhilarated. I never do things by halves. When I do fall in love, I fall hard and totally, giving my all to the man. I could never be casual about love or sex. I would feel too used by someone who didn't care about me as a person. I could never be just a lay. There's nothing in that for anyone. It leads to feeling worthless.

Love inspires passion in me. I want to give my all, do anything for that person, especially physically. I love every inch of a man then. I can touch and look at him for hours; it's as if I can't get enough of him. I like to think of him, talk to him, and share with him. I'm more interested in giving than receiving. Still, I don't expect him to make me happy. Happiness comes from within. You need to accept yourself and be a person in your own right before you can offer anything. You have to find your own meanings in life. No one should shoulder the responsibility of being the only person in your life.

I don't like silent lovers. I want to know my lover's thoughts and feelings. I want him to tell me how he feels before, during, and after sex. I get such a thrill from this. I always want the room to be light so I can read passion in my lover's face, and so he can feel good watching my responses. I love the closeness, the caring and sharing of people at their most vulnerable, most human self, with all their defenses down. It's a fantastic feeling to be that intimate with someone. It's wonderful when two people can trust each other enough to bare themselves emotionally.

It's almost what D.H. Lawrence calls "burning out the shames" in *Lady Chatterley's Lover*. When Lady Chatterley is speaking of her experiences with Mellors, she says something like, "She had come to the real bed-rock of her nature and was essentially shameless." At that point, she has nothing left to disguise or to be ashamed of because she's shared her ultimate nakedness with a man, another human being.

My affair with Pat came close to that. It was refreshing and extremely intimate and showed me what was lacking in my own life. Growth is always painful, but not to grow is not to be alive. I discovered much about myself over the past few years. For a relationship to continue both parties have to change. I could never go back to conditional love or love on someone else's terms. That is selfish love; it implies that the self, the conditions, are stronger than the love.

My affair occurred as a result of marital problems, and needs and desires that weren't being met within my marriage. My husband was so busy with his own business he had little time left for me. I felt lonely, undesired, unloved, and neglected. I never felt noticed, let alone appreciated.

A few years earlier I had fantasized about other men whom I flirted with, but I never pursued the idea. I felt guilty about even thinking like that. I thought a commitment was a commitment. But flirtation was a good boost to my morale. When my affair started I was unhappy, but I didn't know what was wrong. I was at a home show when I met a man with whom there was a powerful, mutual attraction. Pat was a great guy with a terrific sense of humor and a *joie de vivre*. We also had a great deal in common since he worked in the same field as I did. Although nothing happened, I hadn't had so much fun in ages. When I got back home I couldn't get Pat off my mind. I began to feel as if I had no control over my emotions. I felt I needed to do something to sort out these feelings. I decided to drive to Pat's hometown and sort this out. I was nervous when I got there, but I went to Pat's office anyway. He was surprised, but delighted to see me. He suggested we go out to dinner since his wife was out of town visiting her sister. I felt more thrilled than guilty.

I took a room in a hotel. I felt decadent, crazy, and nervous. I bought some rum and Coke and had a drink before he came over. We had a few more drinks when he arrived. He was an easy man to talk to. I broke down and told him how attracted I was and how confused I was. He suggested that it was natural and that if I had feelings for people I shouldn't be afraid to show them. He took my face in his hands and told me to cheer up. He wanted to take me dancing because he thought I needed a good time. That was all it took for me. Here was a warm, understanding man who was so kind and considerate, and I was so goddamned lonely. I asked him to just hold me. He told me he'd love to hold me. Before I knew it we were kissing and caressing each other and it felt good to be cared about. I was frightened of what we had started, but I didn't want to stop. He was afraid to take advantage of me because I was so depressed and confused. But I also felt wonderful knowing that someone desired me. Soon, of course, we made love. He talked all the way through about how beautiful I was, how good in bed I was, and what he wanted to do to me. He couldn't keep quiet and I didn't want him to stop talking. His face was tender with desire and pleasure. I remember saying to him that this wasn't the wisest thing to be doing, and he said it was probably the dumbest thing ever.

We made love all night, with about three hours' sleep. He held me tight when he slept as if he never wanted me to go away. We made love in every position; we couldn't get enough of one another. He suggested we become lovers and told me how much he liked me. I stayed four more days and we made love all the time. He told me how easy it was to love me and how he could make love to me for days. He told me funny stories about his sex life. He was fun, and I loved to listen to him.

I felt awakened, alive, beautiful, and sexy. We both wanted to do everything to each other. He told me he thought of me all the time I wasn't there. I felt about twenty years old, yet womanly as well.

We remained lovers for about six months and grew fond of each other. For about three months my own feelings were deeper than Pat's, because my need was greater. I thought about him a great deal; he was a gentle, loving hook to hang onto. We always talked about all our problems. These were very personal feelings. I finally felt needed. Someone was offering himself to me, not holding back, but trusting me with his hidden desires and needs. I wasn't afraid to be myself. I felt as if we'd known each other for ages. Finally I was communicating.

The affair helped me survive the frustration and loneliness at home. It made me realize my husband was a workaholic, too interested in getting ahead to give me what I needed.

Although Pat was married, his wife wasn't interested in sex. We both needed to feel wanted and appreciated and have the marvelous freedom to explore each other sexually. I felt relaxed because I could be myself. It was great to be so open and honest. Pat made me feel like a sexy lady, and showed me what was missing in my life.

I loved the attention and affection and the knowledge that someone found me special. I was hard on Pat, clinging to him like a life raft to keep from going under. Eventually I did leave my marriage, but not because of the affair. The affair showed me I needed fun, emotional warmth, and sharing. After a few months, I no longer needed Pat for security. I regained my self-confidence and found some breathing space to rediscover myself as a person. My times with Pat were fun, and I still regard him as a good friend. But the freedom to be myself overrode all other considerations. I needed to be complete within myself.

After the affair with Pat ended, I delighted in looking around and meeting other men. I reveled in having fun and sharing good times with them. I thrived in my own freedom. I also realized that I didn't need a special man to have fun.

For the past year, I have had a special lover. The man is in his late twenties, easy-going and fun to be with. We each suit the other's needs in the relationship. Given what I learned from Pat, I am able to be a better lover and friend. I also have the moxie to manage a relationship with an attractive, younger man. At the moment we are debating whether to live together. It is a big decision and I'm not sure at this point that I am ready to make such a sizable commitment again.

Loretta

Loretta is thirty. She has a successful career in advertising. She was unhappily married for eight years, obtained a divorce, and lived with a man for a few years. She is presently on her own.

I wasn't in love with my husband. By the time I had my affairs, we'd been married for five years. We had too many problems, and too many things had gone wrong. I knew it was just a matter of time before I left him.

I was seventeen when I got married and my husband seldom paid any attention to me. He was always out with the boys. He also beat me up several times. I would have left sooner except I didn't know how I could survive—I was young and unskilled and had two kids to support. I realize now that for the entire eight years of my marriage I was dying for attention. I was looking for someone who cared for me and who would show it. When you're not getting any attention at home, it's difficult to tell anyone who pays attention to you to leave you alone.

My first two affairs—both one-night stands—were flops as far as sex was concerned. I was desperate for affection and attention. One of the guys I met at school, and we would go out for lunch or a drink. I enjoyed the companionship. When we finally did decide to go to bed, it turned out to be embarrassing. I don't know what happened, but he couldn't get it up. It was about three in the afternoon, and we hadn't been drinking. Maybe we should have. It was rotten for my ego.

The second guy I met while on holiday in Montreal. We were attracted to one another immediately and although we went out, we didn't go to bed. I ran into him again back in Toronto, and this time we did end up in bed. We were totally incompatible. He didn't do a thing for me. It wasn't good for him, either, since I didn't climax and he was disappointed.

I began to despair. I had never had an orgasm. I never had one the entire eight years I was married. Although I felt some guilt over my infidelity, I felt my husband deserved it. He was a terrible lover. I told him from the beginning that I wasn't getting any pleasure out of sex, and I asked him to try different things. It was another five years before he tried anything new, but by that time he turned me off so much that I felt sick when he touched me. It was too late. I didn't love him anymore, and I didn't care. It had got to the point that sex was so boring I couldn't be bothered. I didn't get anything out of it. It was only for his pleasure. If you have never had an orgasm for all those years, you think, "Why the hell bother?"

The last year we were married we stayed in a cottage in a resort for most of the summer months. My husband would drive up from the city on weekends. That summer I met Phil. We got along quite well, and I was attracted to him. He was single, about thirty, and good-looking. A week later I was in a hotel with a girl friend of mine and I phoned him. I asked him to come to the hotel and have a drink.

He said, "I haven't got any money and I've got a girl friend."

I said, "That's all right. I've got money. I'll buy you a drink."

After that night we began to see each other on a regular basis a couple of times a week. Sexually he was fantastic, an absolute knockout. He knew what he was doing since he had lots of experience. He took his time. It was a wonderful, very erotic experience for me. He turned me on anyway, but he also did things to me that I had never had done before. He was one man who knew what he was doing when he went down on me. He also gave the most marvelous massages; they made me melt all over. He really cared about what I got out of lovemaking. We both had very healthy sexual appetites. I went crazy because I had so little sex in my marriage. We were in bed all the time.

Phil knew I was married and he also knew my husband, and he still continued to see his girl friend. My husband still came up on weekends, but I didn't like to see him. By the end of the summer I decided to stay on at the resort and not to return to the city. When I told Phil, he said, "Oh, no, what do I do now?" I told him not to worry because I had been planning to leave the marriage anyhow. I stayed at the resort and got a job. My husband wanted the children so he took them. I never missed my husband for two seconds, although I felt badly about the kids.

Phil and I continued to see one another. We didn't know where the relationship was going. It could have turned out to be a fling, but in our case it turned out to be something serious. It was also great fun. I was very much in love with him. We ended up living together, and I was the first person he ever lived with. He didn't drop his old girl friend until he moved in with me. Even after he moved in with me he occasionally saw his old girl friend. I didn't like it because she was still hung up on him. I was always afraid he still cared for her, and I had said to Phil I would step out of the picture if he wanted to go back to her.

After about two years of living together, he began to pay less attention to me, and it started to bother me. The last year we were together we only made love about once every three weeks. I always believed he was the type of man who would never be faithful. He had always had a girl friend but he continued to play around on the side. He was so used to having a variety of women that one woman was boring for him. I figured he would end up screwing around on me. I knew he had screwed around a few times. Our sex life began to go downhill. I wanted to marry him, but he could never make up his mind. I left three or four times during the last year, and he always talked me into coming back by promising we would get married. When I moved back in I never heard another word about it.

That last year we were together I missed the attention, the sex, and the love. I'd go to work and cry. I couldn't trust him. Once men have a pattern like that it's hard to break. I was extremely frustrated. Finally I moved out permanently.

I do still like relationships that are exclusive and long-term. I like the security of a relationship. Now I look for sincerity and trust in a man.

8 Evelyn, Joey, and Karen

Evelyn

Evelyn is a thirty-nine-year-old brunet. She is now separated from her husband, who is a university professor. They were married for fourteen years. She has done many things in her life: taught, worked in public relations, and worked in the art world.

My husband and I had very little sexual experience when we were married. My husband was a virgin; I had lost my virginity in a one-night stand to get it over with. Although I had a liberal, progressive marriage in most respects, my husband had a nineteenth-century attitude toward sex. It was one of the only things we didn't talk about. I was very curious sexually and I wanted more experience. After about six years of marriage, while we were living in Europe in the early seventies, I started having affairs. I found affairs really helped my marriage because I could bring the experience and those good feelings back into the marriage. The affairs freed me sexually and my sexual insecurities vanished. The affairs had a positive effect on my relationship with my husband because I became more secure within myself.

For years I never understood why my husband loved me. I had been overweight and thought of myself as a cerebral rather than a sexual person. I always felt I attracted people by the qualities of my personality. The year we moved to Europe was the year of my coming of age as a sexual, physical human being. That year I was twenty-seven, and both my husband and I had been doing a great deal of heavy drugs. I lost twenty-five pounds in a very short time. It was the first time in my life that I was not restricted by a job, or by my own culture.

When I began to realize men were attracted to me just physically and saw me as a sexual person I was flattered, but extremely frightened. I had a change of attitude within myself; I began to feel attractive. I think affairs don't come along unless you're ready, and by that time I was ready because of my changed attitude and circumstances. It was as if life were unfolding as it should.

At that time my husband also went through a crisis. He came to me with a fellow he had met at work and they confessed they were attracted to each other and wondered what I thought of them getting together. My husband was on the verge of coming out of the closet and admitting he was gay. Although I had sensed something was wrong, I hadn't consciously realized he was gay. I felt this had nothing to do with me. And if he did have an affair with this man, it would not detract from our relationship. I never imagined he would run off; our marriage seemed secure, too solid and too supportive. I believed nothing external could threaten us. We were always the best of friends. My husband did not pursue his first gay relationship.

My first affair was with an American man in Europe, a man we had known in the States. Rod and his wife were in the process of separating and his wife had left to go back to the U.S. Rod wanted to travel across North Africa for a few months, and asked me if I would be his traveling companion. My husband didn't object. He told me to go and have a good time. Although Rod and I had not slept together before the trip, we never ruled out that possibility.

Inevitably, because we were together and became friends, we did have an affair. Our relationship was similar to the one I had with my husband. We were open and trusting and supportive of one another. The first time we made love was after we had both dropped acid.

The entire affair was wonderful because we both felt totally liberated. We were in a strange land and away from everyone we knew. Most of my sexual insecurities were dissipated by my relationship with Rod, and I had a reaffirmation of myself as a sexual being. My first affair was so different from my first lay. Rod was much more knowledgeable and sensitive on all levels, and much less lustful. It was good because of the freedom, the experimentation, and the experience of being that close to another person. It lasted for six weeks, until the trip was over. He cut the trip short because he was haunted by his wife and still very much in love with her.

I told my husband about the affair. He didn't mind because neither of us was jealous and the affair didn't interfere with or threaten the marriage. I was able to share all this new knowledge and bring new techniques and freedom back into our marriage; it made our physical relationship that much better.

I had three other affairs during the time I was married. They were all nice and all different. One was a fantasy come true. My husband was out of town, and I ran into a man to whom I'd always been attracted. He asked me what I was up to and I said, "No good!" I was really on the make. We had an affair that lasted several weeks, but it got rather messy. My husband arrived back from Europe sick with hepatitis. He was angry because he had never liked this man, and because other people knew about the affair. He viewed himself as a cuckold. He was so sick I couldn't explain anything to him; he was quite horrible and unreasonable.

Another affair was great because it was so dangerous. The man was my best friend's lover. No one ever found out about that one. Our closeness grew out of a friendship. It was not love at first sight, but something that built up.

I also had several lesbian experiences. The first one was easy. We were both new to the experience, and it was more curiosity than lust. I was experimenting and trying to satisfy my curiosity. The others were with friends, and the experience was a natural outgrowth of the friendships.

My last affair was a catalyst. My husband had come out of the closet and was going to the public baths several times a week. In the homosexual world, "physical" is the operative word. There is more sexual freedom there than in the heterosexual world. I was frustrated because I couldn't experience things I wanted: the mores of society were prohibitive. Because I was someone's wife, many men thought there was no possibility of an affair. I had to be the aggressor. People were always concerned that they were cheating my husband.

My last affair was a fairly intense one, with another artist. I was working with him and seeing him three times a week for three or four months. Through him, and an art exhibit we were working on, I learned a lot about myself and creative expression. I was pushed to my limit in all directions and I learned what my capacities were. I was freed artistically, as well as freed forever of any sexual inhibitions. Both the art show and the affair became so intense and held so much that life became very stressful. I felt I was close to a breakdown because of the pressure.

I separated from my husband shortly after that and for three years I had no relationships. During those three years I was very reclusive. Finding myself and my art became more important than contact with another person.

I enjoyed all my affairs. I gained experience, satisfaction, and understanding. I asked questions and got answers. It was wonderful to communicate and be so intimate with others. I felt great because I felt more of everything and I was aware that my partner was feeling more, too. At one point or another I was definitely in love with all the people I had relationships with.

There was always more than sex to every affair. There was always friendship. I've never understood how women can go to bed with someone they don't know. I don't know how a woman can feel free enough to have an orgasm with a stranger. But I loved extramarital sex. It was always more frank, more straightforward. It was never obscured by day-to-day routine. It was outside of the usual and I always learned something new. I learned how different people were. I love to learn new things and I love to be surprised. I also experimented sexually because I felt free to experiment. I felt I couldn't liberate my husband without liberating myself first.

Now when I look for a man, I look for sincerity, trust, and understanding; I look for someone who is rational and interesting.

Joey

Joey is thirty-six, small, slim, and attractive. She was married for nine years and had one child before she divorced her husband. She now lives with a lover and her daughter. Today Joey is the owner of a successful small business.

I had a lot of space in my marriage, but I never abused it. Until the last six months, I never considered the possibility of fooling around. When I decided I didn't like marriage any more, all kinds of things happened.

My first affair started because of a girl friend who was incredibly brave. We were both married and we thought we were happily married, yet we were looking to have more fun in life. The two of us and two single girl friends used to go out to bars once a week for a night on the town. Occasionally men would proposition us. We loved the flattery.

One night when we were out, my girl friend and I started

talking about the idea of taking a holiday without our husbands. The more we talked about it, the more we liked the idea. I still didn't realize I was unhappy with the relationship between Paul and me, but the idea of two weeks alone in Florida was appealing. We told our husbands we wanted to go and they trusted us.

Down in Florida I went out on a date with this hunk, a Michael Landon type. He was the suave, debonair kind. He was also single. I didn't know anything about single men. Within half an hour we wound up at his place. He came on to me and tried to stick his hands down my pants. I didn't have to be experienced to know he was a pig, but he didn't scare me. What upset me was that such a gorgeous guy could act like such an animal. He made it evident to me that I was nothing to him. I found the thought disgusting. I made him take me home.

When I got back to the motel room I found my girl friend and the pervert's chum. The chum had given my girl friend a joint. We had never smoked grass, and she thought she had died and gone to heaven. I went to the bar. During the week I had developed a good rapport with the bartender. We had instant communication, and we became chums. While I was at the bar, my girl friend phoned me and asked me to come back to the room because she was "freaking out." I said to the bartender, "Why don't you come over after work? We're going to be leaving in a few days." I was just being friendly. He came over about midnight and we ended up in the sack all night. The whole night was exciting because I'd never even had a shower with a man. Even to kiss another guy at that time seemed exceptionally romantic. After that night I was so excited and exuberant I thought I'd been reborn. I also thought I was in love. It had been so easy—I guess because we were away from home and excited about the trip.

A romantic like me really gets overwhelmed, but what good would life be if you didn't taste it? Having an experience like that really whetted my appetite. It made me realize what I was missing. Making love to a strange man when I had only had sex with my childhood sweetheart made me realize there was a vast difference between one man and another. After nine years of marriage, my husband was not exactly pole-vaulting to get to me. The bartender was panting and purring, and I couldn't believe it was all for me. It was a real turn-on and it took me a long time to get off that high. That was the beginning; I began to look around. It was a little like losing your virginity. Once it's over and done with, you open a brand-new door; you are a new and different person.

When I returned from Florida I had my second affair. By this time I wasn't very thrilled about being married, and when an opportunity came along, I took it. I went to a party where I met a cop. He was twelve years older than I was, very handsome and very strong on his own values. He was at the party with his wife and kids and I was there with my husband and my daughter. I realized that he liked me. He gave my girl friend his phone number and asked her to have me call him. I called him, then met him around the corner from my house. We went out of town to a sleazy bar. We ended up making love in the car that first night. It was certainly chemistry. It was very intense and very strong. I felt fabulous in every way. It was like falling in love for the first time. But I think I was falling in love with myself, more than with the guy. All of a sudden I was an adult with opportunities. I felt worldly.

The affair became very intense, and I got involved with his family and his life. It was a filthy mess. His wife—one of my chums—was running around, and I would go out with her and pick up other men with her. It was really tacky. She had a strong suspicion I was involved with her husband. His kids were crazy about me, and they used to say they thought their father was running around. It got to the point where I hated myself for the whole sticky mess. This went on for about a year, even after I left my marriage. I wondered how I would get out of it, prevent all the pain. His wife called and told me she and the kids knew. They didn't like it, but no one took it to heart. It was my sense of guilt that made me give up the relationship. I felt disgusted with myself. I had other opportunities— there was no point in screwing up their relationship. I have avoided married men since. Affairs with married men are more like love affairs because married men are much more romantic. They're so glad to have contact with someone. When you're not out and about in single land, no one owes anyone anything.

Six months after I returned from Florida, I left my marriage. I realized that, for me, having a relationship with another person meant I didn't want to be with my husband. Once I accepted that my marriage was over, I was overwrought. I didn't know how to get out of it. My husband and I had come from broken homes and we had a youngster, so I felt guilty. I thought, "God, my kid's going to come from a broken home, too."

My husband and I never talked about my affairs at the time, but years later he told me he knew, and he told me of an affair he had had. A friend of mine once told me she had the hots for Paul. I told her to help herself, and she did. I was hoping she would have an affair with Paul because it would relieve me of some of my guilt. I felt I deserved it. When you're screwing around you think your spouse is true blue, but that's just ego. All of a sudden you feel all the attention is on you and you distort reality.

There were reasons beyond my affairs that made me leave my marriage. I had always had a lot of responsibility since I was a kid. By the time I had a husband and child I felt I had spent my whole life looking after people. I needed a break. I didn't mind being responsible for myself, but I could see that Paul wasn't going to get that far in life. Paul has always been an adolescent; he'll never be a man. I've done ten times more with my life than he has done with his. I lost respect for him. He would have hampered me. Once that feeling overwhelmed me I began to realize I couldn't stand being married to him.

The world was exciting when I left my marriage because it was the first time I could experience new men. Since I was fifteen I had only gone out with my husband; I had confined myself to a narrow life. Many people approach freedom with fear instead of looking at it the way I did. I was like a little kid going on a holiday. For the first time in my life I didn't have to answer to anybody and I didn't owe anyone an explanation. Many people aren't used to that kind of freedom. They get scared and can't let go of their past lifestyle. They think the transition has to put them exactly back where they came from. The people who don't have enthusiasm don't appreciate freedom. There's nothing more attractive to a man than a woman who is in love with someone else, because she's not paying attention to him. When you're independent it makes a man feel he wants to be around you because you're a challenge. He wants to know how to break down your barriers.

There was always more than sex to any relationship I've had. I like men and I like to relate to them. I couldn't be in the company of someone who wasn't interesting on a social level. The beauty of a person is in his personality. My worst fear was being intimate with someone who did not approach life with honesty. I didn't think of myself as a one-night stand, but once in a while I would meet a man who would fool me—he'd end up being very shallow. I'd wind up feeling stupid for letting him use me. I know I'm smarter than that. But you learn to contend with this. You become better able to make decisions about who you want to be involved with, what to expect from certain people, and you learn to stay away from things you can't handle.

If I could have had three men rotating on a regular basis that would have been perfect. I didn't think then I would ever give up being single. Three men would have satisfied my ego. If you can't have men on a regular basis then you feel abused. It's difficult to attract lovers. A lover is someone who becomes your steady lay whether it's once a week or once a month. A lover is someone who has some form of commitment to you. It's difficult to find someone who wants to incorporate you into his lifestyle.

Just because a relationship isn't fulfilling and doesn't satisfy you forever doesn't mean that relationship isn't worthwhile. You've made an impact on another person's life and that opportunity comes to you because it's something you have to offer. I am a little chunk of all those people I've had experiences with. Sometimes in relationships I would realize something was missing, and rather than hanging in there, I'd get out. There is no point in just hanging in. You make a move. Quick decisions are also a part of success in anything.

If people were less sober about life, we'd all be a lot happier. People get caught in the drama. The more you are able to handle, the more you gain. Many people stop themselves and look at the reasons they should or shouldn't do this or that. I couldn't stand the thought of knowing I'd wanted somebody and that I had never checked if he wanted me. I wouldn't be satisfied if I hadn't made the attempt. I couldn't stand to sit back and let life pass me by. Looking back on the associations and the opportunities I've had, I wouldn't sell a minute of it, even the times I made mistakes. I think I am who I am because of all my experiences, and I like what I've become.

Over the years I've developed a better understanding of what I desire. I don't want an ordinary relationship: I want a relationship that keeps my creativity alive and gives me an extreme high. If I hadn't found it, I would have settled down. It wasn't that I wanted more than anybody else; I just knew exactly what I wanted. I now have a definite idea of what I expect from a man. I don't have the same aspirations and ideals I had before. I don't want to be on my knees begging to kiss his feet. A woman without my experience wouldn't demand the type of respect I demand. But I feel I've earned respect. I've earned it from my ability to stand alone. I've paid for it by having to take burdens on myself.

Sexually I was pleased with my husband; he was my teacher. I was always raring to go, but he would pick the times. With lovers I received a lot more attention, because lovers are horny all the time. In terms of physical satisfaction my husband was one of the best lovers I ever had, because there was a lot of exploring. Not too many men know what they're doing. They talk about it a lot, but when it comes to doing it they don't have a clue. For most men sex is at the end of their dick. They think all they have to do is get hard for you. They don't realize that sex is sensuality. I never had that problem with my husband; he was a very sensitive man.

Once I got over the ego trip of being wanted when I was fucking around, I found most men were really inadequate. Most men don't make love through their hands or their mouth. Most men talk about going down on a woman; they've heard that's what they're supposed to do so they act as if that's what they like. But the ones that talk the most about doing it usually don't. You can tell when a man is a lover or a boaster. I would guess about seventy-five percent of men make love to satisfy their egos, and the other twenty-five percent are fucked up. What does that leave you with? A woman trains a man to be a good lover. Any of the long-term relationships I've had have been that way.

In the long run, once you realize your ego has been more than satisfied, short-term affairs become boring. You want to have relationships that give you more, and that you can work at. If I were to go out with someone now, I would be much more aloof and detached. My fiancé gives me many of the things I went without for a long time. With him I have camaraderie and respect. I like it because I feel fulfilled. If I hadn't matured, I wouldn't have appreciated Tom. While I was single I found everyone shallow. People only related to me on a sexual level. Men's wants were very physical and once they got you they didn't want you anymore. They were all childish and confused. I had to be a good game-player. I was too honest and too blunt to play games for very long. That's why I was ready to settle down with Tom.

I did, however, have a chance to fulfill all my sexual fantasies. Ironically, they were all instigated by Tom since he had been my chum throughout the entire ten years I was single. I had a flaming love affair with his twenty-one-year-old nephew because I had always wanted to make love to a younger man. The turn-on was that he was so gorgeous and so sweet and in such total awe of me. I was in complete control: I knew everything and he knew nothing. But I knew the affair would only satisfy me temporarily. The reality lived up to the fantasy and I'm grateful I squeezèd it in.

A *menage à trois* was another fantasy of Tom's and it marked the point we became lovers. My girl friend and Tom and his friend were all chums. We raced around like kids. Often we'd do strong dope and then we'd all sit around and rub each other's feet. One night the two fellows and I came home stoned and Terry started rubbing my feet while Tom rubbed my back. Before I knew it, all three of us were in the sack. It wasn't dirty or gross; the three of us were just playing. I trusted them because we were all such good friends. I thought it was great, but by the end of the week I couldn't stand it. I told the guys the kick was over and if it carried on I would feel cheap. Although we had fun, I really found I liked Tom more than Terry. The reality was actually better than the fantasy because I never thought I would be in a position with two men with whom I had such good rapport and whom I trusted so much. After that, Tom and I became lovers. We've been together ever since. Now Tom has to deal with it because he instigated it.

I'd never have affairs now. I've had enough experience to know I'm not missing anything. From a sexual point of view I'm not going to get anything better than what I can develop at home. I'd rather develop love at home with someone who deserves it than with some shmuck out there. Few other men have given me the respect, admiration, and appreciation that Tom gives me. When I see a gleam in some guy's eye, I know some other person is going to get the same gleam. Very few people who are available are sincere. But if you started out looking for the right man you'd never have any fun.

Karen

Karen is twenty-four, tall, with long brown hair and large brown eyes. As a teenage mother she gave up her child for adoption; she finally married the child's father, but they separated two years later. Karen studied accounting and now has a good position with a brokerage firm.

I met Ted, my husband, when I was young and naive. Ted appealed to me for all the silly adolescent reasons. He was wild, appeared uninhibited, and drove a Trans-Am. I was terribly hung up on him for so long it was pitiful. I had built him up in my mind to be something he wasn't. I was quite a romantic, and I was starry-eyed about him.

We got married because of parental pressure. After we were married, I realized Ted wasn't very mature. He changed even more when we moved to a small town. He didn't like having the responsibilities of a house and a wife, and he missed all his buddies in the city. There was no communication between us. He spent most of his time watching sports. I got little attention or affection. I also need physical warmth, and he couldn't provide it. We didn't make love for months at a time. I hate to say it now, but I begged my husband to make love to me. I began to feel I wasn't loved.

Although my husband and I did a lot of experimenting, I was never able to come. Finally I did have an orgasm, but I needed oral sex and manual stimulation with intercourse. During the time I was married I faked orgasm a lot. I also found that although Ted turned me on, I needed to fantasize about women. I was turned on by the women in *Playboy* magazine and I still didn't realize at the time that I might be gay.

During that first year of my marriage, I had my first affair, with a guy I worked with. He was gorgeous and he drove a sportscar. I think I have a sportscar fetish. This guy was moving out west soon and a group of us went out after work for a bon-voyage party. After the party he wanted to drive me home, but we ended up making love in the car, right in the parking lot. For the next two weeks I went over to his place every day after work and we made love. I was infatuated with him; I thought he was wonderful. I ate up all the bullshit about being wanted. He made me feel like a million bucks. Although I never had an orgasm with him, I needed physical warmth and I needed to feel desired. Somehow I also had the crazy notion that the affair would make my marriage terrific because I would feel so much better. But, by comparison, the way my husband treated me seemed that much worse.

My second affair was with a friend of Ted's and mine. Ted and I had spent many evenings with this guy and his fiancé. It was during this friendship that I realized I was really fond of women. I fell in love with Janet, Wayne's fiancé. I also knew Ted was interested in her, too. Up until then, although I had all these fantasies of women, I still didn't realize I was gay. But if I had known I wouldn't have had the guts to come out of the closet.

I spent ages planning a whole scenario to seduce Janet. I thought if I got close to Wayne, I could get close to her. I suppose I envisioned some kinky foursome, where in the end I would get Janet. I also knew Wayne wanted me. One night when I knew both Ted and Janet were busy, I invited Wayne over. I put on a negligée. It wasn't long after Wayne came over that we made love. He was really ready for it. Unfortunately Ted and Janet never did get together. I finally told Janet how I felt about her. Although I know she wanted to go to bed with me, she was too straight. It actually got messy because the night before Janet's and Wayne's wedding, Wayne phoned me and wanted to come over. Talk about backfiring.

Soon after that Ted and I separated. I went back to the city and went to school. I got in touch with all the guys I considered both Ted's friends and mine. Every one of them asked me out. They had all put me on a pedestal. I went out with five guys a week for six months and I slept with all of them. But they all wanted more than sex; they wanted the big romantic number. They wrote songs and poems for me. At that time I was still confused about my sexuality and I didn't want any emotional involvements. My biggest fear was that these men would fall in love with me.

I suppose I went out with all of them because I had to convince myself I was desirable. With men I always felt inadequate, since I was uptight about my body. I had stretch marks on my breasts and a large vagina due to childbirth. It took a number of men to convince me I was adequate. But I was always very submissive and passive with men, and that really wasn't me; I'm really more aggressive.

Finally I decided to do something about my lesbian tendencies, but I knew of no place for lesbian women to go. I eventually contacted a group for gay women in the city. These women had a lot of integrity and they really wanted to help. Many of them were professional women who got turned off by the kind of men they were meeting. They also really liked women. I felt very comfortable with them because I could relate to them. With none of my other friends had I ever felt comfortable or fulfilled. Here I felt normal for the first time since I had been a child. Your sexuality touches the very core of your being. Finally I was free to express my sexual self.

At the meeting I met a woman who was quite butchy looking. She was thirty-seven, had never been married, and had never had intercourse with a man. She had the greatest smile in the world. She lived with another woman, but her roommate went out with a man. I had my first lesbian affair with her. It was great. I never had so much fun in my life. She introduced me to a whole underground world of gays where I felt I really belonged. Sex was great with this woman. There was more fun and more kissing. It was light-hearted and pleasant. I never worried about my performance during sex with her. There was more love and body language because we were both on the same wavelength. Yet I still fantasized about other women while I made love to this one. I also liked being able to be aggressive, which I couldn't do with men.

During the time I was with women, I became very much of a feminist and didn't want anything to do with men. Other than Janet, Wayne's wife, I never felt any romance for a woman. I grew to love the woman I had my first affair with, but I wasn't in love with her. I feel emotionally close to women, and I feel sexual chemistry with them.

I am out of that feminist stage now, and I have relationships with both men and women. I have a boy friend who is away at school at the moment and he knows I like women and accepts it. I get just as horny with men, but I don't necessarily need to come. Being bisexual is confusing; sometimes I feel neither fish nor fowl. However, I've learned to accept myself.

9 Joyce and Margo

Joyce

Joyce, who comes from a middle-class Italian family, is fifty. After being married for many years, she is now divorced. She lives in Vancouver.

I think too many ideas about relationships come from movies. Everyone is looking for Mr. Perfect or Mrs. Perfect. No one is supposed to have bad breath, pass wind, or urinate. Are you supposed to stop during intercourse to go to the bathroom to pass wind? No one is looking for real people; what they're looking for is a fantasy. Perfect people don't exist. Not many women appreciate relationships. They're all looking for the stud with the big muscles and the big penis. What good is a big penis? You can have the most fantastic lover in the world and it won't turn you on. Passion comes from the heart, not from someone else's body.

What destroys relationships are the *Is* and the *mes*. People are concerned about their own egos and their own wants. The *I* destroys love. When we say "I" and "me" we lose our sexuality. Sex is giving. Why do people get married and then chip away at each other? People are so selfish and self-centered.

Many people don't know how to give love. I feel sorry for someone who has never loved.

We are all busy playing roles. People are afraid to be honest and show their emotions. They play-act. I hate the whole idea of macho. Acting macho is prevalent among North American men, and it means judging people by their big cars and big muscles. Why can't men be weak and women strong? Why can't a woman have a man just because he's a good partner in bed? Why does he have to be everything else as well? I don't know who sets these standards, but I don't need them—I relate to people from the heart.

I finally managed to shed my Italian Roman-Catholic background, which had made me feel guilty about my sexuality. I used to hide my sexual desires and try to curb my sexual appetite. Good girls didn't go out and pick up men at bars, and nice girls weren't sexy.

My grown son said to me, "Mom, you are the luckiest woman I have ever met. You're so free. You say what you want, and you do what you want. Other women may have their big houses and their big cars, but what good does it do them?" My son's right; they're bored and trapped. Do you know how many women have to take tranquilizers just to get through the day?

Time is a luxury. I don't have time at fifty to play games. That kind of behavior is for superficial people. I have to spend so much time doing what is necessary that I don't want to spend my time with superficial, trivial people. I spend my time doing what I enjoy with people I enjoy.

I've had some fantastic love affairs. I loved my lovers and they loved me. I have only one affair at a time and I give everything to that person, sexually and emotionally. I always remember my relationships. Why do people try to forget them? I still have a lingering love for these men. I care about all of them. They are part of me and part of my life. Forgetting them would be like forgetting part of my life. I feel a bond with all of them, except my husband. Every love was different and I loved them all for a different reason.

Every affair I've had has been fantastic because I've acted on my feelings. I took each one for what it was, and each one was just beautiful. Some men were better lovers than others. An old friend used to say, "There are no bad lovers; some are just better than others."

I try to find something new in every relationship. I love the thrill of an affair. I don't feel marriage is the answer for everybody. Just because someone is married doesn't mean he or she is secure. Signing a contract and saying "I do" does not bring fulfillment. People expect other people to make them happy.

My husband was an adequate lover. I told him I had no sensation in my breasts, but lots of sensation in my back and neck. He didn't care. I insulted his male ego because I criticized his style of lovemaking. He said, "That's the way I make love." He couldn't take criticism and I couldn't build up his male ego. Eventually we stopped talking and the marriage disintegrated. My last child was a love child from a special night with my husband when we tried to get back together. That night was the first night I was really sexually aroused and the first time I climaxed. The attempt at reconciliation failed, although we continued to live under the same roof. My husband was an old fart at thirty, and now he's an older fart at sixty.

The last year we lived together I was working in a beauty shop in town when a big Irishman who had been clocking me for ages came into the shop and asked me out. Although I refused his advances for a long time, I finally said yes. I don't know what I was saving myself for. I told my husband I was going out with him. I didn't feel guilty.

The Irishman turned out to be a fantastic lover, although he was an alcoholic. We spent much of our time together drinking. When anyone said anything about me, he always defended my honor. He was tall and experienced and the affair was fun. We had some crazy times.

The affair was the final straw in my marriage. After five years of marriage I took the kids and moved out into an apartment of my own. I had to be tough and independent to survive and raise three boys on my own. I've become aggressive, and aggression is threatening to men. A woman doesn't have to be masculine to get what she wants. I'm attracted to very masculine men, but I believe it's because I like to be dominated. If men are smart enough they can dominate me without saying a word. Many of these men don't even appreciate their own masculinity.

The Irishman was very masculine. My affair with him lasted twelve years and we were still good friends when he died.

My second affair was with Bert, and it lasted twelve years, too. This affair ended because it burned out emotionally.

After the relationship with Bert, which broke up two months ago, I met two men. Peter, who is seventy-four, is just a friend and a wonderful man. Peter is intelligent and I enjoy our conversations immensely. People ask me what I'm doing with such an old man. He doesn't seem like a man of seventy-four. My husband seemed older at thirty. Peter is gentle, easy-going, secure in himself, and he doesn't need his masculine ego boosted. He's a gentleman and mentally stimulating. When I'm out with him, I feel proud to be with him. He gets a lift from being with me—I think I make him feel younger and stronger. People in our society slough off older people and treat them as if they don't exist. I love Peter dearly, but I wish he were ten years younger. Sometimes I say things that hurt him because I am more agile intellectually. He just accepts me. I'm in high gear and I wish at times I could slow down for him.

The second man I met and with whom I'm having an affair is Darcy, who is a few years younger than I am. He has a dirty mind and I love to hear all the stories about his other women. I tell him I'm glad he knew all those other women because I'm reaping all the benefits of his experiences. Darcy is gentle, tender, and warm, but he is a weak man. He's the nicest man in the world when he is sober, and his lovemaking is stupendous. But when he's drunk, he smashes things and becomes evil. His alcoholism is a sickness. At forty-three he has done everything and has nothing to look forward to. He became jaded because he never had to struggle.

I don't know what I'd do if I wasn't loved. Being unloved would be terrible. There's never been a time in my life when I haven't been loved. People grow old when they aren't loved and don't love. Love is in the giving, not the taking. It is beautiful to love. You give warmth and caring, not just sex. Sex is the ultimate act of giving. You give part of yourself. It is the closest act. I would never waste the time or effort just to fornicate.

I've never had an affair where I didn't climax. I love my partners and they love me, and I've never come unloved. If I ever had a relationship without love and caring I would be destroyed. Caring means getting to know about another person's body, being interested enough to find out what makes him tick, what creates his passion. To be used as a sexual object would be an insult to my femininity and my womanhood. I couldn't sink that low. I've never entered that kind of relationship because it would be destructive.

In the very act of sex, we give our all. We reach out to people and want to shower them with all our love. If I'm making love, I'm making love to someone I care about.

When I'm in love, I love to have sex. I've become a very earthy person. Exploring different bodies is great. Men love being fondled, touched, and loved. If you give your man attention, you get attention back. Sex is fantastic. Sex cleanses the system and clears the pipes. When I'm in love, there are no holds barred in sex. I can't imagine sex without fellatio and cunnilingus. The first time I ever sucked a penis, I was aware of the odor and taste. The taste was beautiful because it was part of the man. When I'm in love I love giving someone pleasure and happiness.

One day with Darcy I was overcome by wanting to give him something to make him happy. We were driving along the river at about dusk and I pulled the car over. I was overcome by a desire to make him happy. I gave him a blow job in the car, even though there were other cars driving by. I'd never done anything like that before, and I'll probably never do it again. The experience was beautiful for both of us. Darcy almost collapsed.

A wonderful Jewish woman I knew years ago—she must have been seventy-five, but she still painted her nails and wore Dior dresses—told me you have to be a whore in your heart and in the bedroom, but a lady in public. Men like to see both characters in a woman: the virgin and the whore.

I have no regrets about my life. I've had a fantastic life even though I've had my hardships. I've wanted to die many times, but I've pulled myself out. Some people can't take life. I've prayed at times. If you've got to give your troubles to somebody, it might as well be God. I like being right where I am. I never wish to be any younger.

Margo

Margo is of Irish heritage. She is in her mid-thirties and comes from Michigan. She had a working-class background and is nominally a Catholic, even though she is divorced.

Like almost everyone who grew up in the States during the time of JFK, I guess I developed a sort of social conscience. I didn't want to become a nun. I used to hate the nuns because I got spanked a lot in school. I sure couldn't become a priest, and I didn't think I wanted to join the Peace Corps and go off to India. So I ended up joining VISTA.

After the training period, I was assigned to a Blackfoot reservation in central Montana. I was like a junior social worker, a sort of visiting homemaker.

Despite my Catholic upbringing, I always thought of myself as a sexually active person. The kids I grew up with in Saginaw were a fun-loving bunch. We slept around with each other, but no one ever got hurt. I always told myself that those experiences would help me find the right guy; you know, Prince Charming. I just knew that without good sex, there couldn't be a good marriage. If I'd stayed a virgin till I got married, like my mother did, how would I ever know?

As they say out west, there was "slim pickins" on the reservation. Obviously, there were Indians, but the desolation and frustration of their lives made them alcoholics before they were old enough to drive a car. It was depressing. The only other people around were a priest and a couple of guys who worked for the bureau of Indian affairs. Unfortunately, while these guys were great beer-drinking buddies, they were all happily married and had no intention of cheating on their wives. It was six months after I started working on the reservation that I met Billy.

Billy was a Blackfoot who had moved to Detroit, where he'd got a job in construction. There was a long strike in the building trades and Billy figured he might as well wait it out with his family in Montana. We hit it off immediately; he was tall and strong and seemed to be laughing all the time. He looked like the sculpture on the front side of a nickel. He had a savage tenderness in bed that made me beg for more. He would hold me so tight that I would have bruises on my arms and body, yet he kissed me so gently.

Six months later, we were married and I left VISTA and moved with Billy back to Detroit. It was divine; we were very much in love. At first my parents were furious with me for having married an Indian, but eventually they came around, even though I didn't get invited back home for all the family get-togethers. I didn't care—I had my man and I was happy.

About a year after we were married, there was a big slump in the building trades and Billy was laid off. In the beginning, there were no real problems. His unemployment insurance covered most of our needs and I was able to get a job. After his unemployment ran out, my working was the only source of income, and I imagine his pride was hurt.

We lived in that part of Detroit that some people call Fort

Apache; nothing but Indians living there. Billy would grab my pay as soon as I got it and hit the bars. He'd boast about the dumb squaw he'd married and buy rounds for everybody. When his money—it was really my money—ran out, he would come home drunk. My life was pure hell during that time.

Billy had been so strong and now he was weak. He just wasn't the same guy I'd married. We would still make love, but the tenderness was gone. I was beginning to feel like General Custer every time he took me to bed. He was rough.

I had my first affair at that time. An old friend from my hometown came down one day, and we literally ran into each other. There was a hotel across the street and Ken suggested we go there and have a drink.

Ken was a godsend. I was at the lowest point in my life. When he got around to asking me what was new, I burst into tears. He was strong and reassuring as I told him the sorry state of my life. Ken had a room at the hotel and suggested we go up there. I agreed because I felt like a damn fool sitting in the bar and bawling.

There was a bottle of Scotch in his room, and the two of us began hitting it hard. Within an hour, Ken had me laughing again. I knew I should be going home soon to Billy, but I couldn't bring myself to leave. It had been too long since I'd been happy.

I don't know how it started, but after a while, we were kissing each other, then touching, and finally our clothes were off and we were fucking. There were no promises and no commitments; it was just plain old dirty fun. About the time I had finally forgotten about Billy, and we were about to have our second fuck, Ken noticed the bruises on me and asked about them. Boy, did that bring the curtain down.

I fumbled with an explanation, but it was too late. I always like fucking twice in a row; I always think the first time belongs to the man and the second time is all mine. Not this time, though. Every time Ken thrust into me, I thought of Billy, and that I'd have to tell him what happened. I figured he'd understand.

I got back home around seven that night. Billy was drunk, as usual. I poured us both a drink and told him that I had to talk. I explained what had happened that afternoon and that it didn't mean a thing to our relationship. I told him I needed a break, and it was a coincidence that I ran into Ken. I told Billy that I loved only him, and I knew times would get better for us. He was silent for a while, but I just couldn't believe he was upset with me. After all, Billy had confessed to me about all the affairs he had had. I knew he had to prove his manhood at every opportunity. But I knew he loved me. I still loved him, and it was unlikely that I'd have an affair again.

Finally, he just smiled and asked me for some money. He wanted to have a few drinks with his friends. I gave him twenty dollars. As soon as he left, I took a bath, a long, slow one. Then I got a book and read myself to sleep. I was enjoying the sleep of the contented because I'd had my little fling and I'd told Billy.

I don't remember what time Billy came home that night. He was roaring drunk, but I didn't consider that unusual. He burst into the bedroom, and started yelling that I was a whore, white trash, and a lot worse. He pulled me out of bed by my hair and began to slowly slap me around, each slap a little harder than the last. I was so stunned I couldn't scream and I think that made him even angrier. He began punching me. I don't remember how long he kept it up. I guess I blacked out; I'm not sure.

Then he dragged me to the living room where his brother and two friends were. Suddenly, his brother had his pants off and he started raping me. I tried to fight back. I tried to scratch his eyes out, but Billy punched me again. When his brother came and when there was no response from me, Billy kicked me in the ribs. Then the other two raped me, too, and all the time the physical and verbal abuse continued.

I left Billy the next morning and went home. When my parents saw me, they were hysterical. I lied to them and told them I got mugged. I just had to get away from the city. It took me nearly a month before I could tell my mother part of the story and she helped me with all the legal stuff. The grounds for my divorce were mental cruelty.

I've gotten married two times since then and each time gentleness was the major factor. When my second marriage was ending, I had a couple of affairs, but I never told my husband.

If my marriage is happy in every way, I don't need to have an affair. Once it becomes clear that it's over, the affair just becomes an escape, a link with sanity and a way to get myself prepared for the new world I must face.

Have I got any advice for somebody having an affair? I sure do. Never tell your husband! Even if he's got pictures, deny it. As soon as your husband discovers you've had an affair, he changes. He can be the sweetest, most gentle and understanding guy in the world. Tell him about your affair, and you're liable to get beaten.

10   The Art of an Affair

Popular mythology has it that when a political scandal rocks the English-speaking world it involves sex, but when a scandal rocks France, it involves money. While this probably is not true, it certainly illustrates the North American belief that the French are more worldly about sex than the rest of us. Justified or not, they enjoy the reputation of having raised the management of their affairs to an art.

When we think of the French, we imagine leisurely relationships that last for years with a special day and a special time set aside for lovers; quiet rendezvous and long, romantic luncheons; husbands who are tolerant because they're having affairs of their own, and wives who look the other way because they know the occasional fling makes their husbands better-natured. We certainly never associate ugliness with the French; they're too sophisticated for that.

The perfect affair does not exist, of course, in France or anywhere else. But if it did, surely this is what the ideal liaison would be like—romantic, leisurely, civilized. If a woman is already having an affair or if she knows she is headed for one, how can she ensure it will have at least some of these characteristics?

The first and most obvious prerequisite is the right lover. Where do women find their lovers? The women interviewed for this book all met their men in one of three ways: by proximity, by design, or by pure coincidence.

By Proximity

Men and women who work together often have affairs because of their proximity to one another. People who share the same working environment get acquainted slowly; normally they already know quite a lot about one another before the affair begins. Unlike people who are dating, co-workers are under no pressure to socialize for several hours at a stretch. Instead, relationships are free to develop more naturally. And co-workers also have the advantage of a mutual interest and a ready-made topic of conversation—their jobs. A woman may go home excited about something that has happened at work only to find that her husband really is not interested. It is natural for her to turn to another employee to discuss business; if she keeps doing this, she may eventually find she has more in common with her co-worker than with her husband.

Co-workers also tend to see each other when they are at their most attractive. At home, the married man may always be dressed in worn jeans, a paint-stained shirt, and slippers that have seen better days. Perhaps he doesn't bother to shave on weekends. And he always seems tired. By evening, he's collapsed into a nonverbal state in front of the television. But on Monday morning that same man is clean-shaven, smells of cologne, has combed his hair, and is immaculately dressed in a crisp white shirt and three-piece suit. He's rested and he's all smiles. Is it any wonder his female colleague finds him attractive?

By the same token, women in the office are also groomed and dressed to perfection. Co-workers may know each other in many ways, but seldom have they seen each other in what might be described as the natural state.

Just as people tend to look their best at work, they also tend to be on their best behavior. The man who is short-tempered and shouts at his wife at home knows that he can't behave that way in the office with his secretary. There are too many people around to witness any displays of temper. And so the man who is a pugilist at home is often a diplomat in the office. His secretary or female colleague thinks he is always interesting, good-natured, and tactful. And he may always be—provided she doesn't marry him.

At the most practical level, work also legitimizes a woman's contact with her lover. Very few women want to get caught. A woman whose lover is a co-worker can see her lover regularly, go out for lunches, and perhaps attend out-of-town functions without making her husband suspicious. And communication is simpler: there is no need to rely on the telephone—so there are no mixed-up messages and no fear of calls at the wrong time.

But if affairs in the work place have their advantages, they also have more than their share of drawbacks. The major one is office gossip. Whether a woman is actually having an affair or merely carrying on a flirtation, there will likely be gossip. It survives on innuendo, chance remarks, and the special, nonverbal relationship lovers have. Even two people who think they are discreet may give themselves away by how close together they stand, by how often they touch, and in a hundred other ways. Very few people enjoy being the subject of gossip; those who want to keep their affairs with co-workers secret will have to be especially careful.

Another drawback is that management generally frowns on affairs between staff members, especially when those staff members are married to other people. If the company is a conservative one and the affair becomes obvious, it is likely to be the woman who is dismissed. Like it or not, there is still a double standard. Boys can be boys, but nice girls must watch their step.

Finally, it is often more difficult to end an office affair amiably because you must continue to see one another. If your lover ends the affair, and if he is your superior, you may find yourself transferred out of his sight. If you are the one who ends it, he may continue to pursue you. And if you are at all uncomfortable seeing him, or worse, if you have started to loathe him, then the situation will be impossible.

Proximity also comes into play when women fall for friends of their husbands. Many of the women interviewed suggested that they had affairs with friends whom they had known for years. Such affairs often have the potential to be hurtful and destructive.

Patricia's story illustrates the problems: "I've been married to Jack for seven years. We have a good marriage and many interests in common. We also have three small children.

"For the last three years, Bill and Sally have been our closest friends. They have four children, each a little older than ours. We've gone camping together—kids, pets, the works. Twice a week we meet and play cards and then last year just the four of us went off for a vacation in Acapulco.

"Sally and Jack wanted to go out on a catamaran. Bill and I stayed on the beach and talked, tanned, and drank piña-coladas.

"At first he just commented on how well Jack and Sally got along and how good it was that Jack could sail because Sally loved to sail and he always got sick. I agreed, because I'm not much of a sailor either.

"Then Bill kept edging closer to me, lighting my cigarettes, being really attentive. I felt really attracted to him and when he started to come on to me, I guess I wasn't really surprised.

"We finally got up and went back to the hotel and made love for more than an hour and a half. It was erotic and even though I found myself praying it would be terrible, it was anything but. Looking back, I guess we were both terrified that Bill and Sally would come back, just throw open the door and find us there naked on the bed. We were so damn scared we were both over eager, but there was this real fear of discovery that gave the sex an added dimension.

"We didn't get caught, but we both felt guilty as hell. At dinner when Jack and Sally were dancing, Bill said, 'It's about time the two of us got it on.'

"I started crying and said, 'The two of us! There's four adults and seven kids involved.'

"Bill just nodded and that was the end of that."

Friends and those related by marriage are often attracted to one another because they grow to share common interests and experiences. When young couples spend a great deal of time together, they grow fond of each other's partners. They get to know one another well; they see one another in relationship to their spouses; comparisons are easy to come by. Sometimes young couples mutually decide to "swap partners," and if everyone is agreeable, such relationships may work. But such agreement is hard to come by among four people, and one partner may feel forced into such a relationship, or deeply hurt by it.

Affairs between close friends and those connected by marriage can produce severe distress for the participants. An unhappy example is provided by Irene.

Irene was divorced and admits that she was lonely, missed love, affection, and a sexual relationship. She had no men in her life and she lived in a small town where it was difficult to meet men, especially as she had three children and had to stay home with them.

Irene's sister and brother-in-law used to drop in often, to visit and to make sure Irene was all right. Occasionally, Irene's brother-in-law would come alone, and stay to have a beer. Eventually, these visits became more intimate and Irene and her brother-in-law began necking and petting. Irene responded to the attention and the physical warmth. After a time, she and her brother-in-law began making love.

Irene was literally sick when she realized she was pregnant by her sister's husband. She had an abortion and ended the affair, and although no one ever found out, she says she continues to feel sick, guilty, and haunted by the whole episode.

The dangers for friends who become lovers are obvious. Friends are often a part of the larger network of those who are close, and the relationship may have ill effects for others who are also loved.

By Design

Not all affairs just happen. In some cases, women who are bored at home or want to pay their husbands back for being unfaithful decide to have an affair of their own. Singles bars are the most obvious haunts for these women. Many of the people interviewed mentioned them and, indeed, from the numbers of married men and women in singles bars, it is obvious that their designation is something of a misnomer.

Here are two very different comments on the bar scene from two women who were interviewed.

Susanne: "Don't be misled by the 'Goodbar' syndrome. If every woman who ever frequented a singles bar became a pincushion for a maniac, the bars would have closed years ago. Use your street smarts. The first time, you might want to go with a friend who knows the place; the second time you can go alone. There's an amazing number of men on the prowl out there."

Lonnie, on the other hand, didn't like singles bars. Her comment is the opposite of Susanne's.

Lonnie: "I was looking for someone interesting and genuine. I wanted sex, but I also wanted someone I could talk to afterwards. All I found in singles bars were morons."

Clearly, the bar scene is not for everyone, but just as clearly bars do satisfy a certain need for some women.

A woman who cruises bars probably has to have certain characteristics. She must know the kind of man she is looking for and she ought to have the aforementioned "street smarts." Essentially, this means being able to ask questions within the normal course of conversation and being a good judge of character. She must also be outgoing. She has to have a certain amount of self-confidence and she has to be master of rejecting the unsuitable and encouraging the suitable. A singles bar is no place for a shy woman who isn't used to drinking. It is a place for an experienced, outgoing woman who knows how to handle herself and her liquor.

There are many kinds of singles bars. Some have a warm, friendly atmosphere; there is dancing, and the bars serve almost the same purpose as a community center. Others are just plain sleazy.

The main disadvantage of the singles bar is the fact that you will be dealing with strangers. It takes more than a few drinks to get to know someone. Under the influence of alcohol, it is easy to make a mistake. There is also the question of motivation. It is assumed that a woman alone in a singles bar is there to find a bed mate. A union whose first and final object is sex is unlikely to develop into a long-lasting, warm and friendly affair; nor is it likely to have the romantic qualities many women say they are seeking.

Frequenting singles bars may result in feelings of rejection, or in a series of unsatisfying one-night stands. The singles-bar scene is not for the woman with severe emotional problems; it is for the happy, outgoing hedonist who has developed the same love-'em-and-leave-'em attitude projected by many men.

By Coincidence

Coincidence places many people in our pathways and when two people accidently meet and they are both looking for something similar, a chance encounter can turn into an affair.

The wild life of the traveling salesman is probably exaggerated, but many women claim to have met their lovers in similar ways. One met hers when her car broke down and another motorist stopped to help. The motorist, who drove her downtown while her car was towed away, turned out to be the most eligible man she had met in months. They ended up having lunch and exchanging phone numbers; their relationship developed from their chance meeting.

Others have met their lovers in doctors' offices, during

intermission at concerts, and at corner grocery stores. Janice met her lover in a most unusual way: she was eating lunch in a local cafeteria and she spilled her entire tray over him, dousing him in ketchup, onions, and a soft drink. Naturally, she had his suit cleaned. When she delivered it to his apartment, they got to laughing about the whole incident. One thing led to another. Janice has been a confirmed klutz ever since.

Much of the lingo of modern sex is related to sports. "Did you score?" "Was it a home run?" "Touchdown!" Love may be nothing in tennis, but it appears to be a real enough score in the sex match. Many of the women interviewed met their lovers in sports clubs. This, they claim, is where to find the body-beautiful clique.

Many women also claim to have found lovers while squiring their children to and from assorted sports activities.

Diane explains how she met her lover: "My two children belong to a swim team. Going with them is time-consuming and demanding because there are so many meets out of town. There are long hours to kill between ten in the morning and ten at night. I met Ray at a swim meet. He comes from another town, but we kept running into each other at these meets. Boredom resulted in our having coffee together; we used to talk for hours and eventually ended up having a long, comfortable affair."

Married Men Versus Single Men

A married man who is looking for an affair usually has one of two reasons: he is seeking variety, or he is unhappy. He may also be vengeful, in which case he should be avoided like the plague. If a man is intent on having an affair to get even with an unfaithful wife, then the woman he sleeps with is the instrument of his revenge and not his consummate lover.

Married men, like married women, also have obligations to home and family. The woman who has an affair with a married man can only expect to be a very small part of his life. She must be willing to accept that role, and if both partners are married, the complications may be enormous. Essentially, it means scheduling the affair with two families in mind. If the affair deepens and the couple decides to have a permanent relationship, the result can hurt two families.

Two married people seeking an affair outside a marriage may have quite different motives. Unhappiness is an emotion that varies from case to case. Two unhappy people may find comfort with one another, but both partners should be cognizant of the basis of their relationship. Comfort is comfort; it is not necessarily love.

One advantage married men may offer is that they do not usually publicize their sexual liaisons; for that reason, a woman whose lover is married is less likely to be caught. For the married woman, however, the single man unquestionably presents fewer problems and fewer complications. To begin with, not so many people are involved; there are no wives, and only her own children or in-laws to consider. The married man may have commitments; the single man will be better able to accommodate the married woman.

Whatever a woman does, she should not count on marrying her single lover if she leaves her husband. Single men may not want to form a long-term relationship. Often they have not remained single easily, but are what we might call "woman-wise." They know how to elude the net of marriage (one of the reasons they have affairs with married women). The woman who fantasizes about divorcing her husband to marry her lover should seriously consider her own motives. Is she being realistic? Is it really another marriage she wants?

One last word: for the married woman, the happy wanderer is undoubtedly the best choice for an affair. This is the man who is looking for a casual, fun-loving relationship, not an intense liaison. If he is married, the happy wanderer probably keeps his wife perfectly contented—along with numerous other women. If he is single, he probably has several women on the line, and they probably all think he is wonderful. The happy wanderer is not out to pay anybody back; as a result, he is likely to be both discreet and honest with you. If you do not want anything permanent, an affair with him might be ideal.

The Ages of Man

The age of a man and his status makes each affair unique.

Young and Anxious: Under Twenty

Seventeen-, eighteen-, and nineteen-year-olds combine innocence and emerging sensuality. They are little boys and men simultaneously and they bring out both the mother and the lover in many women.

A young man is not usually an experienced lover, but women often enjoy initiation rites and there are benefits for both parties. Eagerness and enthusiasm can, in some cases, substitute for skill and experience.

An older woman can look to a younger man for physical stimulation, but if she is bright and well-educated, she may find a younger man callow and boring. Young men also tend to brag, and if they are bragging about you, their indiscretion could have consequences.

Desire Under the Elms: The Twenties

Men in their twenties are often idealistic and romantic as well as sexually potent. They may lack experience, but they are old enough to appreciate a teacher. An experienced woman will be in control, while a man in his twenties is in awe.

Younger men are active and not yet tied down with careers;

therefore they show up more at community activities. Yvette, forty, met Ross at a symphony rummage sale, and she thought he was the best bargain there. Ross was twenty-five, sweet, humorous, gentle, and caring. He brought her flowers each time he came for a visit.

The biggest problem with men in their twenties is that they are sometimes starry-eyed and can easily be hurt. It is gratifying for a forty-year-old woman to know that her twenty-two-year-old lover adores her and wants her to leave her husband to marry him, but she will have to let her young man down very easily when she tells him their relationship is just a pleasant diversion. And if an older woman starts to give in to her young lover's romanticism, she is liable to find herself in real trouble. A May-December relationship will sometimes last for a few weeks or even a few months, but seldom will it last for more than a few years.

The reverse is also true, of course. More than a few women have been hurt by callous young men. Lee's twenty-year-old was dynamite in bed, but he had a short attention span. He would go out for a chocolate bar and forget to come back to her.

Up and At It: Twenty-eight to Thirty-eight

Up and at it, but the "it" is not you. This is a difficult age for men. Many are totally wrapped up in business and are too busy to be adoring romantic partners. A great many more men in this group have already had unfortunate sexual experiences and are wary of women. There is no question that the sexual revolution, which has resulted in sexually aggressive women like Tina and Claudia, has bewildered and frightened many men. They appear to be as worried about the woman who is liberated and aggressive as they are about the stereotypic clinging vine.

Many women complain that affairs with men—especially single men—in this age group smack more of business arrangements than of love affairs. This is also an age group with a high divorce rate, so it is logical to assume that business interests affect sexual relationships within marriage as much as they do outside of marriage.

But these are general impressions, and not every man in this age group is wrapped up in business.

This is also an age when a man discovers he has married a boring wife, a woman who has failed to keep step with him intellectually. At this age, men, like women, begin to look around for diversion: women they can discuss business with, women who do not always have a headache.

For the right kind of woman, the man in this age bracket can be a joy.

The Staid: Thirty-eight to Forty-eight

Men in this age group are more comfortable with themselves than men in their twenties and are usually secure and self-assured about their sexuality. Nonetheless, some are of the old school and have serious reservations about the equality of women—especially aggressive woman.

Most men in the upper end of this age bracket have achieved a modicum of success in business and are no longer looking for intense ego rewards. They tend to be slightly more caring and settled; usually they are ready to make an emotional commitment to an affair. They may also offer stability and security. Since many are divorced, the possibility for a strong attachment exists.

Moira's affair with a man of forty-seven ended because her lover came to rely on her for all the affection, attention, and caring he was not receiving at home. He envisaged her in his life somewhere in the future and he dreamed openly about a number of his fantasies. The pressure on Moira was great: she did not desire a relationship of such intensity. Her lover, however, was truly a lover in the total sense of the word. He fulfilled her needs on many levels.

The Young at Heart: Forty-nine and Older

Charlie Chaplin was well into his sixties when he married seventeen-year-old Oona O'Neill, daughter of playwright Eugene O'Neill. They had a number of children; the last one was sired when Chaplin was in his eighties.

Many women have fears about the male climacteric (male menopause), but such fears are largely unfounded. The man older than forty-nine is usually a slow and deliberate lover, exactly what most women claim they want. Older men also love to wine and dine a lady, but the key word is *lady*. They tend to be conservative about what a woman should be and how she should behave.

Many women overlook older men because they are afraid these men can't father children. But biologically, a man produces new sperm for each ejaculation, while a woman is born with all her ova. Thus, it is women who peak biologically at thirty-nine, not men. Men can have happy, healthy sex lives and produce happy, healthy children for a long time.

Both men and women can enjoy sex after the climacteric; women often enjoy it more after menopause even though they can no longer produce children.

There was a time in North America when elderly people in senior citizens' homes were kept apart from one another, but today, more and more members of the medical association are recommending that staff keep their morals to themselves. If two eighty-year-olds are found cuddling, you can be sure they'll make it to ninety.

Setting the Stage

As we all know by now, sex has more to do with the mind than the body. If a man is tense because of frustrations at work; if a woman is preoccupied with a sick child, it does not matter what opportunities for sexual gratification are placed before them. They aren't going to be interested because their minds are on something else. And if they do have sex, chances are the lovemaking is not going to be particularly satisfying.

Both men and women have been led up the pathway of rising sexual expectations. A great deal of misinformation and exaggeration in the media has caused severe feelings of failure among members of both sexes. Many articles and books, for example, have been written about the elusive vaginal orgasm. Sex manuals galore reproduce pictures of people contorted into hundreds of uncomfortable and possibly harmful positions. The purveyors of "magic spots," twenty-four-hour orgasms, and so on all seem to be suggesting that we humans are an incompetent lot who have obviously not been making love properly. They promise more, more, more, with the result that many people who were quite happy now seem to believe they are doing something wrong, or at the least, not experiencing all there is to experience.

What are sex manuals good for? They are an excellent source of stimulation for the mind, and it is the mind that counts most in the art of lovemaking.

The Role of Fantasy

Helen is married and she talks happily about the night she had a one-night stand with her husband. He was running a conference for executives in a large downtown hotel and was provided with a suite. Alas, Helen was not a registered hotel guest, and thus could not stay overnight in the suite.

Her husband laughingly suggested she come down around eleven at night for a couple of hours, and Helen did. By the time she had sneaked past the desk clerk and reached her husband's room, she was feeling like a hired call girl.

Having his wife show up late at night, her nightgown in

her purse, triggered a fantasy in her husband's mind. Where sex had been routine a few nights before, it was hot and torrid in the hotel suite. Conclusion: both their minds were engaged.

One hotel in California caters to fantasy lovers. Each of its rooms is decorated in a different theme, either geographical or historic. Many couples come bearing their own costumes in their luggage to make their fantasy complete. The guests can have their choice of a Henry VIII suite, a Western suite, a Spanish suite, a French suite, an Oriental suite, or a modern suite with a waterbed that has controls for lighting and music. The owners and designers of this movie-set fantasy hotel have probably saved more marriages and been responsible for more successful affairs than Masters and Johnson ever dreamed of.

Common fantasies include sex in the park or some other public place like the beach; sex in a haystack; in the boardroom at work; and so on. Setting the stage for a sexual liaison implies selecting a locale where you can both be comfortable and relaxed and where your fantasies can flourish unencumbered by mundane reality.

The ordinary hotel room is where most lovers end up if both are married or if the single one has a roommate. Hotels and motels do not usually object to unmarried couples, and contrary to popular opinion, you break no laws if you both register under your own names. But few people who are married and having an affair want the evidence of a registry slip. Thus they lie and use a false name, or both use the name of the single party.

Traveling in disguise and telling lies make most people uncomfortable, and renting a motel or hotel room every time you want to be together is costly. If you do check into a hotel, try to select one that offers something unusual: an indoor pool, a sauna, or a waterbed. If your lover is single and lives alone, you have no problem, save the fact that your sexual liaison may become routine.

Let's face it: if two people want to get together, they will find a place to do it—whether it's in a hotel, a car, a boat, or on a deserted beach. The one point to keep in mind is privacy. While anything goes between consenting adults, it is not legal to engage in sexual activities in public.

Foreplay

An integral part of setting the stage for an affair is foreplay. Not sexual foreplay; that comes later. Psychological foreplay is part of the game, and it is almost as important in setting the scene as is choice of locale. It might include preparing dinner together in your lover's apartment, going to the theater, or having a romantic lunch in a quiet restaurant. Both partners ought to be engaged in the art of seduction.

To understand fully what is meant by psychological foreplay, let's examine the ever-popular romantic novel. In such novels the hero and heroine come into contact often, but there is a degree of resistance involved. The entire plot is built around the breakdown of that resistance and the climax literally occurs when the two are finally united. A romance is usually some two hundred pages of psychological foreplay. With the right attitude and the right atmosphere, an affair can progress in the same way. Affairs, like marriages, deserve a period of courtship.

When the psychological foreplay is over, the sexual foreplay begins. Some women claim to enjoy soft music during the physical prelude to lovemaking; others find discussions of fantasies help arouse them and their partners. Still others enjoy looking at magazines such as *Playboy* and *Penthouse* or books such as *The Joy of Sex*.

A woman should tell her lover what she enjoys in the way of sexual foreplay. She need not come across like a schoolteacher; instead, she can say in a low voice, "Yes, I like that." By the same token, a woman should discover what her lover likes. The closer two people can come to fulfilling each other's fantasies, the better the sexual liaison is likely to be.

Exploitation

Exploitation is a buzz word used when people talk about sex. Many women, and no doubt many men as well, genuinely feel exploited. The women interviewed speak constantly of feeling "used," and often they speak of being "used" by uncaring husbands. Conversely, these same women do not feel "used" in most affairs, even if those affairs are one-night stands that result in little more than sexual gratification.

Married women can feel "used" for a variety of reasons, but discussions with them indicate that the primary reasons stem from their roles as wives. A married woman is expected to keep the house and look after the children; to prepare meals and to make life easier for her mate. When appreciation and communication cease, she senses that her sexual role has become little more than a convenience to her husband. She perceives that she is to be ready for sexual activity at his convenience, just as she must have the coffee prepared in the morning for his convenience. When she seeks sexual gratification from a stranger, there is nothing else involved. She does not feel used because she sees herself as taking as well as giving. The perceptions of what the marriage has become may or may not be correct, but those perceptions can make a woman feel exploited.

No field of study is more complicated than the field of human relations; no human relationships are more complicated than those involving sex. Sexual relations involve the human ego on the most vulnerable level. Men are no less vulnerable than women, but women are vulnerable in a different way for several reasons. One reason certainly involves the view and role of women historically, but even those liberated from the past cannot reject the pure physical differences between men and women. During the sex act a woman is physically penetrated; many researchers and psychologists have speculated, probably correctly, that women feel differently about sex for this reason. When a woman allows a man to penetrate her, she is giving of herself in the most intimate way imaginable. She desires appreciation, affection, and love in return. When these are not present, she feels physically violated in a way men find hard to understand. She feels used.

In spite of this difference in feeling, women can and do use men sexually and emotionally. The ideal relationship exists when both parties know themselves and each other and understand the parameters of their affair.

An affair that does not result in someone else's misery is ideal. Regardless of how old your lover is, regardless of whether he is married or single, here are some questions both of you should answer.

1. Am I becoming involved in an affair to get even with my spouse for being unfaithful?
2. Do I need affection more than I really desire sex itself?
3. Do I desire sex in and for itself?
4. Am I looking for a short-term relationship and nothing more?
5. Am I in a distressed psychological state, hurt because I feel unloved and unwanted?
6. Do I fear discovery?
7. Deep down, do I feel people should have sex only with their spouse?
8. Do I feel dirty or used every time I engage in sexual activity?
9. Do I feel that casual sex is all right if both partners are aware that it is just that—casual sex?
10. Could I admit to having "used" a man in the same sense I feel that men "use" women?

If you answered yes to numbers 1,2,3,5,7, and 8, you may need a marriage counselor or a therapist. If you answered yes to questions 3,4,6,9, and 10, you are likely to treat affairs casually and to be relatively untouched by them. You also will try not to hurt your spouse.

If a woman goes to bed with a man for sexual gratification only, and he goes to bed with her for the same reason, neither party has a right to feel used. Equality between the sexes is the most misunderstood concept of our time. It does not imply that women can regard men as men have regarded women for so many centuries. It means that men and women have regard for each other.

Are You Headed for an Affair?

The women interviewed came up with these warning signs. You are probably headed for an affair if:

- You dream or fantasize about making love with other men, even though you've never had an affair.
- You find yourself flirting with other men, and it makes you feel good all day.
- Your husband pays as much attention to you as he does to a fence post; your lovemaking is infrequent and you find it unexciting.
- You find yourself reading romances or watching soap operas and wishing you were the heroine.
- You start to envy your single friends and all their escapades.
- You find yourself deliberately trying to look sexy.
- You have more fun when you go out without your husband.
- You find you want to go out all the time.

If you want an even better barometer of whether you are likely to have an affair, try the following quiz.

Quiz

Choose only one answer for each question. Each answer has a specific point value. Total your points when you've answered all the questions and see how high you score. The point values are listed at the end of the quiz.

---

1. Age?
   - (a) 17 to 24
   - (b) 25 to 34
   - (c) 35 to 44
   - (d) 45 to 57
   - (e) 58 and older

2. How long have you been married?
   - (a) Less than one year
   - (b) One to three years
   - (c) Four to seven years
   - (d) Eight to ten years
   - (e) More than ten years

3. Number of marriages?
   - (a) One
   - (b) Two
   - (c) Three
   - (d) Four or more

4. Occupational status?
   - (a) Housewife
   - (b) Employed
   - (c) Self-employed
   - (d) Unemployed

5. How many children do you have living at home?
   (a) None
   (b) One
   (c) Two
   (d) Three
   (e) More than three

6. How often do you have intercourse with your husband?
   (a) Every day
   (b) Three times per week
   (c) Once a week
   (d) Less frequently

7. Does your husband satisfy you sexually?
   (a) Yes
   (b) Most of the time
   (c) Some of the time
   (d) Not at all

8. Do you and your husband experiment sexually?
   (a) Regularly
   (b) Occasionally
   (c) Seldom
   (d) Never

9. Do you consider yourself good in bed?
   (a) Yes
   (b) Most of the time
   (c) Sometimes
   (d) Not at all

10. Do you masturbate?
    (a) Frequently
    (b) Occasionally
    (c) Seldom

(d) Not at all

11. How often do you go out socially with your husband?
(a) Frequently
(b) Occasionally
(c) Seldom
(d) Not at all

12. How often does your husband take you on holidays?
(a) Frequently
(b) Occasionally
(c) Seldom
(d) Not at all

13. How often do you take a shower with your husband?
(a) Frequently
(b) Occasionally
(c) Seldom
(d) Not at all

14. Has your husband ever had an affair?
(a) No
(b) Once
(c) Several times
(d) Many times

15. Do you enjoy being in the company of other men?
(a) Frequently
(b) Occasionally
(c) Seldom
(d) Not at all

16. Do other men find you desirable?
    (a) Frequently
    (b) Occasionally
    (c) Seldom
    (d) Not at all

17. Do you flirt at parties?
    (a) Frequently
    (b) Occasionally
    (c) Seldom
    (d) Not at all

18. Do you fantasize about other men?
    (a) Frequently
    (b) Occasionally
    (c) Seldom
    (d) Not at all

19. Does your husband buy you gifts?
    (a) Frequently
    (b) Occasionally
    (c) Seldom
    (d) Not at all

20. Do you read romances?
    (a) Frequently
    (b) Occasionally
    (c) Seldom
    (d) Not at all

21. Do you watch soap operas?
    (a) Frequently
    (b) Occasionally
    (c) Seldom
    (d) Not at all

22. Do you enjoy dancing?
    (a) Frequently
    (b) Occasionally
    (c) Seldom
    (d) Not at all

23. How often do you go out socially with your girl friends?
    (a) Frequently
    (b) Occasionally
    (c) Seldom
    (d) Not at all

24. How often does your husband travel out of town on business?
    (a) Frequently
    (b) Occasionally
    (c) Seldom
    (d) Not at all

25. How often do you travel out of town alone on business or pleasure?
    (a) Frequently
    (b) Occasionally
    (c) Seldom
    (d) Not at all

26. Which woman do you admire most?
    (a) Margaret Thatcher
    (b) Eva Peron
    (c) Margaret Trudeau
    (d) Jane Fonda
    (e) None of the above

27. Which man do you admire most?
    (a) Burt Reynolds
    (b) Omar Sharif

(c) Henry Fonda
(d) Truman Capote
(e) Bjorn Borg
(f) None of the above

Answer Values:

1. $a = 4, b = 5, c = 3, d = 2, e = 1$
2. $a = -3, b = 1, c = 3, d = 5, e = 2$
3. $a = 1, b = 3, c = 3, d = 5$
4. $a = 1, b = 5, c = 3, d = 3$
5. $a = 5, b = 3, c = 2, d = 0, e = -3$
6. $a = 1, b = 2, c = 3, d = 5$
7. $a = 1, b = 2, c = 3, d = 5$
8. $a = 1, b = 2, c = 3, d = 5$
9. $a = 7, b = 5, c = 3, d = 1$
10. $a = 5, b = 3, c = 2, d = 1$
11. $a = 1, b = 2, c = 3, d = 5$
12. $a = 1, b = 2, c = 3, d = 5$
13. $a = 5, b = 3, c = 2, d = 1$
14. $a = 1, b = 3, c = 5, d = 7$
15. $a = 5, b = 3, c = 2, d = 1$
16. $a = 5, b = 3, c = 2, d = 1$
17. $a = 5, b = 3, c = 2, d = 1$
18. $a = 7, b = 5, c = 3, d = 1$
19. $a = 1, b = 2, c = 3, d = 5$
20. $a = 5, b = 3, c = 2, d = 1$
21. $a = 5, b = 3, c = 2, d = 1$
22. $a = 5, b = 3, c = 2, d = 1$
23. $a = 5, b = 3, c = 2, d = -2$
24. $a = 7, b = 5, c = 3, d = 1$
25. $a = 7, b = 5, c = 3, d = 1$
26. $a = -3, b = 2, c = 5, d = 3, e = 8$
27. $a = 4, b = 5, c = 2, d = -5, e = 5, f = 8$

If You Scored:

25 to 47 points: Your self-image could stand some improvement. Life has given you little, and you reciprocate in kind. You seek security rather than excitement. Chances are you are quick to condemn women who have affairs, believing that they are immoral. You are a seedling who has not yet decided whether to grow or to wither. Once the choice is made, you will either resign yourself to your position in life or flower. Right now, you are certainly not headed for an affair, but with the slightest change in your attitude or lifestyle, who knows?

48 to 68 points: You are definitely on the brink. Irreconcilable factors in your life are now being felt for the first time. You feel an itch, but you don't know where to scratch. You still believe that you're a one-man woman but formerly small problems are looming larger each day. You're working hard to make the marriage a success, but you would appreciate a little help from your husband. No time limit has been set for this assistance. But if it's not forthcoming soon, you will begin to consider new possibilities.

69 to 92 points: Your big toe has been testing the waters, but there is still some reluctance about plunging in all the way. When you go out with your girl friends, you probably allow yourself to dance with total strangers; occasionally you may have even consented to go back to a stranger's place. You enjoy the company and especially the attention you receive from these men, but you hold back at the last moment. Every time this happens, you have a perfectly valid excuse, whether it's not wanting to lie, fear of VD, your period, or that old standby "This is all happening too fast for me. Please give me some time." Unless you get hit by a car, time is about to run out on you.

92 points or more: Either you are living on a desert island alone with the world's greatest lover or all your male friends are gay. If you haven't had an affair yet, it is not from lack of trying. Take that vacation alone you have always wanted. Your husband will probably understand, and you will feel much better.

One question was deliberately omitted from the quiz: "Are you willing to have an affair?" This is the most important question of all, and it can only be answered with a yes or no. This quiz can only assess the likelihood of your having an affair. No matter what characteristics you show, you will not have an affair if you are not willing to have one.

11 Affairs Have Consequences

All human relationships involve the possibility of pain, guilt, anguish, and rejection. Affairs are no different. But in addition to the psychological effects that affairs can have, sexual relationships also carry the danger of physical consequences: venereal disease and pregnancy.

Physical Consequences

Even a faithful wife runs the risk of contracting one or more venereal diseases if her husband is sexually active outside of their marriage. Consequently, every woman, but especially those who are having affairs, should periodically be tested for venereal disease.

The following information is not intended to frighten, but rather to educate. Knowing about VD can help prevent these diseases from spreading; it can also help you avoid an unpleasant experience.

Syphilis

The bacterium that causes syphilis is shaped like a corkscrew; its medical name is *Spirochaeta pallida* or *Treponema pallidum*. Since this bacterium is a spirochete, it can invade all human tissue and is not restricted to the bloodstream.

Syphilis is often called an imitator because its later symptoms can imitate those of almost every other disease.

Syphilis, untreated, has the following stages: primary, secondary, latent, and tertiary.

The Primary Stage: The primary stage is marked by a sore at the place on the body where the bacteria entered. This sore is usually found on the sex organs, but it can also be on the mouth. The sore is called a chancre and, more often than not, it is hard and painless. It may look like a small spot or ulcer and can be as small as the head of a pin or an inch or more across. The primary chancre is often concealed and may not be noticed. It can appear anywhere from ten days to three months after exposure. The average incubation period is, however, twenty-one days. By this time the spirochetes have spread throughout the body. *The disease is highly communicable while the chancre is present.*

During the primary stage, there are usually no other symptoms.

The Secondary Stage: Even without treatment, the chancre will disappear within two to three weeks. The secondary period usually lasts from several months to several years. During the secondary period, skin rashes may appear, the hair may thin, and there may be headaches, pains in the joints, fever, fatigue, and mucous patches. The spirochetes diffuse further throughout the body and can be found in the bloodstream.

Latent Stage: The signs and symptoms of the secondary stage gradually pass away even without treatment. During the third stage or quiescent period, the spirochetes are still present in the bloodstream. The latent period can last from five to twenty years with a full range of two to fifty years being possible.

Tertiary Stage: During this final stage of the disease, syphilis becomes the great imitator. It may attack the brain or the spinal cord; it may attack the heart, the blood vessels, the skin, or the bones. Tumorlike masses may appear, the aorta may rupture, blindness and deafness may occur. Untreated, syphilis is a killer.

Syphilis must be diagnosed in a laboratory. The best-known test is a blood test called the Wasserman test. Once it is diagnosed, syphilis can be treated with penicillin or tetracycline. The treatment is painless and reasonably simple. It does not require hospitalization. For those who are sexually active with a variety of partners, it is not unreasonable to recommend a Wasserman test every four months.

Good hygiene will not prevent syphilis although a condom can prevent a chancre from coming into contact with vulnerable tissue. You ought to know if your chosen sexual partner is sleeping with others, and, if so, how many. A little honesty between the two of you can be beneficial and might save you from the embarrassment of having to tell your husband or another lover of your condition.

If you do become infected, however, it is imperative that you report all your sexual partners to your doctor so they can be notified. When you realize that failure to report all your partners might have serious consequences for dozens of people, you can better understand the responsibility each individual must take.

Gonorrhea

Gonorrhea is the most common of the "social diseases." It is caused by a specific microbe, the *gonococcus*. It spreads from person to person, almost always as a result of intercourse.

The only source of a gonorrhea infection is the discharge from the lesions of the mucous membranes or lymph nodes of a person who is infected. In rare instances, a fresh discharge may live long enough on towels or other bathroom items to cause an infection. Young girls, six or younger, seem especially susceptible to vaginal infections caused by such discharges. These are the only cases of infection that are innocently acquired. Since the mucous membranes of the eyes are especially susceptible, newborn infants are usually treated with silver nitrate drops.

Symptoms

Gonorrhea symptoms appear from one day to three weeks after contact with an infected person. *In the male* these symptoms usually include pain, stinging, and burning when urinating, and some swelling and discomfort in the urinary region. There is also a discharge of some pus (a few drops) from the penis.

In the female, symptoms may not occur. If they do, they can include a puslike vaginal discharge and swelling and possible abscess of the Bartholin's glands, the glands at the vaginal opening. (There can be an abscess or swelling of these glands without the cause being a venereal disease.)

Untreated, gonorrhea continues to progress and can result in sterility, arthritis, inflammation of the heart valves, and a host of other crippling diseases. The diagnosis is made by laboratory test. The treatment is simple and involves antibiotics.

It should be noted that it is possible to contract both syphilis and gonorrhea at the same time and, indeed, from the same person.

Herpes

Two types of herpes simplex virus have been identified. These are: herpes simplex virus type I and herpes simplex virus type II. Type I is associated with infections in and around the mouth—fever blisters and cold sores. Type II is associated with genital infection. Scientists are still not certain whether crossover infections occur, but recent evidence seems to support the theory that they do. Genital-herpes infections are transmitted through sexual contact, and oral-genital sex may be responsible for some crossover infections. Others may be the result of self-infection; that is, you may touch a cold sore on your mouth and then touch your genitals.

Herpes is the fastest-spreading venereal disease of our time.

While no reporting laws exist, authorities estimate that there are as many as 300,000 cases a year in North America and this constitutes an epidemic of monumental proportions.

There is no cure for Herpes II at the present time. It is a dangerous and significant disease. Infants born to infected mothers can be seriously ill; the disease causes discomfort, pain, and embarrassment; and the disease is associated with cervical cancer.

The incubation period for herpes is usually four to five days, but can be as short as twenty-four hours.

The symptoms include: pain or itching at the site of the infection and the appearance of a blister-like lesion (this may be an individual lesion or a cluster of lesions). In a few days these blisters rupture and leave raw tissue surrounded by inflamed skin. At this latter stage, the site of the blisters becomes extremely painful with intense burning and irritation. In women, severe burning during urination is common.

The ruptures take from five to six weeks to heal and recurrent infections are common. In females, the lesions may occur in the vagina, on the labia, the clitoris, the cervix, the thighs, or the buttocks. In men, they can be on the foreskin, the shaft of the penis, and on the glans.

Everyone makes an effort to avoid all diseases, but the diseases spread through sexual contact cannot be completely avoided unless the individual involved practices total abstinence. Since this is an unrealistic suggestion, the following steps can reduce your chances of encountering sexually related diseases.

1. Have a yearly physical examination; include testing for VD and a PAP smear.
2. If you are active sexually with multiple partners, have frequent blood tests.
3. Avoid sexual contact with a person who has any visible sores.

4. Avoid genital-mouth contact with anyone who has a fever blister or cold sore.
5. Practice good hygiene and don't sleep with anyone who doesn't.
6. Discuss VD with your partner.
7. Agree to limit the number of sexual partners you and your lover have.
8. Use a condom if you're unsure (this isn't guaranteed to prevent disease, but it can help).
9. If you contact VD, see a doctor immediately; if you acquire questionable symptoms, have an examination immediately.
10. If you have VD, report all your partners so they can be notified.

Reporting Venereal Diseases

Reporting syphilis and gonorrhea is required by law in most jurisdictions. At the present time, it is not required that herpes be reported.

Reporting of venereal disease is confidential. But remember that if your husband is not having an affair—if he cannot have been the source—he will find out you are having an affair. One gentleman who was sleeping with a married woman reported that his only sexual contacts were the married woman and one other woman. The other woman had a total of ten sexual contacts; the married woman's husband another three. When all the contacts and their contacts were finally contacted, 312 people had to receive treatment.

Reporting is extremely important in limiting venereal diseases; it can also prevent tragedies. Children can be born syphilitic if their mothers have not been treated. If you contract a venereal disease, you must be treated and you must list all your sexual contacts.

Pregnancy

This is the consequence no one wants to think about. It is certainly the one with the most serious implications. Never say "This can't happen to me." It has happened to doctors, to sex-education teachers, to women who didn't know a condom from a freezer bag, and to those who thought they were past it all.

The obvious way to avoid a pregnancy is to use a contraceptive, but this is sometimes easier said than done, for many. Birth-control methods aren't always reliable; sometimes a woman has not planned to have sex in a certain situation and as a result has not thought about birth control; sometimes a contraceptive has been available, but a woman has failed to use it because of recklessness or a misplaced romanticism.

The following is a brief description of the contraceptives available. It is not meant to replace the advice of your doctor.

The Pill

When it was developed twenty years ago, the pill was supposed to free women forever from the worry of unwanted pregnancy. It still is probably the best choice for sexually active women who are younger than thirty-five. It has a very low failure rate and it involves virtually no bother. But more and more women have given up the pill because of its many side effects. These will not be elaborated on here since government agencies supply long warning lists.

The Intrauterine Device (IUD)

These are devices that are inserted into the uterus to prevent pregnancy. Like the pill, the IUD has a low failure rate and, once it is inserted, involves virtually no bother. Unfortunately, some women develop severe cramps and heavy bleeding with the IUD and cannot use it. Most women experience no complications; occasionally, however, an IUD will perforate the uterus. When this happens, surgical intervention is required. IUDs are still undergoing extensive testing.

The Diaphragm and Jelly

The diaphragm is a small, shallow rubber cup that is covered with a spermicidal jelly and then inserted into the upper part of the vagina. When used correctly, the diaphragm is a highly reliable form of birth control with no physical side effects. Some women claim that inserting the diaphragm takes the spontaneity out of sex, but the device can be inserted up to an hour before intercourse. One caution about the diaphragm: it has to be used to be effective.

Foams, Jellies, and Creams

These spermicides are inserted into the vagina prior to intercourse, usually by means of an applicator. While they provide some protection, they are not nearly as effective as the pill, the IUD, or the diaphragm. Many men also complain that they sting or cause irritation. Foams, jellies, and creams are probably best considered a stop-gap measure until a more reliable form of contraception can be found.

The Condom

The first condoms were sheaths made from animal membranes; today, they are usually made from thin latex rubber. Condoms are safe and reliable; instances of condoms breaking and spilling their contents are rare. They are a good method of birth control for casual sex, though most men do not relish their use.

The ideal contraceptive—one that is safe, reliable, no bother to use, and aesthetically acceptable—does not exist, despite the millions of dollars that have been poured into birth-control research. Because certain contraceptives can cause serious side effects, women should be wary of birth control—just as wary as they are about becoming pregnant. But this does not mean they should stop using an effective contraceptive. It is probably wiser to take a calculated risk with the pill than to become pregnant.

Whatever method of birth control a woman decides to use, she should use it without exception during an affair. Women having affairs sometimes become reckless and, like their teenage daughters, rationalize themselves out of using birth control because they do not want to admit that they are going to have sex. Or they decide that if they cannot have a man forever, they want his child. This is a very dangerous attitude. Not only will a pregnancy cause a profound change in a woman's relationship with her lover and her husband, but people have a way of changing their minds. What seems like a good idea in theory may seem very different when a woman is in the throes of morning sickness. Women engaged in extramarital relationships have enough to cope with without the pain and anguish of an unwanted pregnancy.

Abortion

This is one of the most unpleasant choices a woman can make and, when the choice has been made, it is one of the most unpleasant experiences imaginable.

When a woman misses a period, she should not rely on drugstore tests to confirm a pregnancy. These tests can produce negative results when the woman is, in fact, pregnant. A woman who suspects she may be pregnant should go to a doctor and demand a pregnancy test. Even these tests may not be able to detect a pregnancy until two or three weeks after a missed period.

The ease with which an abortion can be obtained depends entirely on where a woman lives. Most women in large cities can obtain abortions without too much trouble, but women in towns and rural areas may have a much harder time. State, provincial, and federal laws also vary, as does policy from one hospital to another. Most hospitals in Canada require that a board of doctors approves each abortion. Obtaining approval during the first three months is easier than obtaining approval later in the pregnancy. In many states in the U.S., abortion is virtually available on demand.

Abortions are relatively simple surgical procedures if they are performed during the first twelve weeks of a pregnancy; after that they become much more complicated and traumatic for the woman. If a woman decides to have an abortion, she should do everything within her power to obtain it during the first three months of her pregnancy.

Some hospitals may require a woman to get her husband's signature on a permission slip before she can have an abortion. This means that her husband will know about the abortion and a record of it will exist. A rare husband will stand by his wife in this kind of situation, but most will not. Usually a woman who decides to terminate a pregnancy will face the turmoil, doubt, and fear alone, without the support of her husband or her lover. And beyond the actual abortion or the decision to keep the child, there are serious questions about financial support.

The best way to avoid an abortion is to beware of your romantic instincts and use birth control at all times.

Psychological Consequences

Guilt

Some women do not feel guilty about having an affair. They may be selfish, they may have arrangements with their husbands, or they may have been able to rationalize their affairs to prevent guilt. But most women do experience guilt to some degree, and it can present problems, depending on how deeply it is felt. A woman who believes her husband is faithful to her while she is sleeping with someone else may feel especially guilty.

Every individual copes with this feeling in a different way. Some women become especially nice to their husbands, some become nasty or contemptuous, still others start to drink, and some may make themselves feel better by confessing.

The best way to handle guilt is to confront it. First, a woman has to know why she is having an affair. Is it just a fling or does it reflect some deep-seated dissatisfaction in her marriage? Then she needs to ask herself all or some of the questions below:

1. Do I feel guilty because I know my husband has been faithful?
2. Do I feel guilty because I still love my husband?
3. Am I being angry with my husband because I'm really angry with myself?
4. Which is more important to me: my freedom or my marriage?
5. Am I afraid of how my husband will react if I confess?
6. Will confessing accomplish anything constructive?
7. Do I fear the censure of my family and friends?

A woman who has had a one-night stand or a brief fling is probably wiser to resist the impulse to confess. Or, if she must confess, she should confess to a friend. A woman who owns up to this kind of affair to her husband probably acomplishes very little except to make herself feel better. And she is likely to make her husband unhappy or angry—all to little purpose. A long-standing affair is a different matter, since it may point to a more serious problem in a marital relationship. In any case, women who are feeling guilty should avoid acting on impulse. Before a woman makes any decision to confess an affair to her husband or to take any other course of action, she should probably talk over her feelings with a good friend or a marriage counselor. At the very least, this will help her put her affair in perspective and decide what she wants to do. Discussing her feelings may also help relieve her guilt.

Broken Marriages

Affairs in themselves do not usually cause marriage breakdown. Marriage breakdown is the result of a) finding a better relationship with someone else, b) a realization of how unsatisfactory the marriage is, c) the reaction of one or both partners to the knowledge of an affair, or d) the emotional fallout that can occur when an affair ends unsatisfactorily.

While an affair may not be the direct cause of a marriage breakdown, it is often the catalyst. An affair sometimes places the marriage and its problems in perspective. A woman who has tolerated an unsatisfactory marriage may have an affair and suddenly realize that other possibilities exist. And so the affair leads to a divorce.

Marriage breakdown causes psychological effects of its own, which will not be discussed here. It is sufficient warning to say that an affair can sometimes act as a catalyst and that marriage breakdown can occur.

12   The Party's Over

There are a multitude of reasons that affairs end: one partner may want a long-term relationship while the other does not. One may demand more time and more emotional commitment than the other can give. One may demand that the other choose between the affair and marriage. One may simply get bored. Whatever the reasons, the warning signs that signal the end are obvious, although people sometimes choose not to heed them. When lovers find they are having arguments over trivial matters, disagreements over the parameters of the affair, gradually drifting apart, or that their sexual relationship is no longer satisfactory, they usually recognize that the end is in sight. In a marriage, people will often try to repair these problems; in an affair, they will generally just move on.

The best time to end an affair is before the two parties have a grand finale. Graceful farewells may be impossible, but civilized breakups should not be out of the question. Women who have ended affairs well say that the best way to conclude an affair is to turn it into a friendship. Such an ending implies that you both still care and value one another as individuals. Even if one partner feels a loss, there is comfort in knowing that warm feelings still exist. The offer of continued friendship—perhaps the offer to see the other person occasionally—illustrates the degree of caring and intimacy that existed during the relationship.

During the course of a special love affair, a woman may reach a point when she realizes the affair is no longer a game or a fling, that it has the potential to affect her life. Many women admit to falling in love during the course of an affair; their lives with their lovers become more important and real than their lives at home. When this happens, they know their marriage is in serious trouble.

It is wise, at this point, to take a vacation from the affair, a cooling-off period. It is advisable to seek out a disinterested third party—preferrably a marriage counselor or a therapist, or even a good friend who has the ability to be objective. The old saying "love is blind," has a lot of truth. In the full flush of an affair, excitement can be mistaken for love. When the excitement fades, many a woman has regained her vision only to realize her lover is either just like her husband or has characteristics that are even less appealing.

A woman who is unhappy with her husband should be especially wary. People tend to exercise the same taste in lovers that they exercised in choosing a mate. It's simply not true that the same mistake can't be made twice.

Lilly's story is a fine example: "When I was twenty-two, I married Sam. Sam was a policeman and I felt he was strong, decisive, and just. I admired his profession and I suppose being married to a police officer gave me an extra sense of protection. I seem to crave the feeling of being protected.

"But Sam and I gradually grew apart. He had to work long hours and I always worried that something would happen to him. He only saw the seamy side of life—dope addicts, hookers, crooks. Sometimes it seemed as if he saw the worst in everyone and couldn't believe anyone was any good.

"Even though our marriage was routine and we didn't talk much, I didn't have anyone else. But he always thought I did. He was always calling to see if I was home, always checking on me.

"Finally, I met Ralph. He was a young rookie cop and very sensitive. We started to see each other and eventually I divorced Sam and married Ralph."

Lilly is now thirty-five and married to her third police officer. Her complaints about her third husband are nearly identical to her complaints about her first one. Lilly not only keeps choosing the same kind of men; she keeps choosing them from the same profession.

An affair, any affair, can serve as an eye-opener. It can illustrate what is wrong with a marriage. The problems were likely evident before the affair, but the woman might have been unwilling to admit the situation because it opened doors behind which were questions such as: If I get divorced, how will I support myself? Where can I go? Will I be alone for the rest of my life?

If these are a woman's fears, then the existence of a lover may give her someone to go to if she leaves her husband. But going from an unhappy marriage into the arms and life of a lover is dangerous. Like Lilly, the woman may find she has all the same problems she had before. Or, once the woman is "free," her lover may reject her.

Wanting a new man before leaving the old one is understandable but immature, and it probably spells danger for the second relationship. All people, not just women, have to learn to be alone before they can become part of a true partnership. The formerly insecure woman whose affair gives her the confidence to leave an unsatisfactory marriage and live on her own has probably benefitted more from her experience than the woman who rushes into the arms of a new lover.

What Do Women Want?

Men have been asking this question for centuries and they have received hundreds of answers. The answers below are drawn from interviews with women.

Women want love. Love is an unfortunate word because

it is misused and ill-defined: it has different meanings for different people. But for our purposes, let us define love as respect, attention, adoration, and friendship.

Women want to be equal partners in the venture of marriage. This does not necessarily mean they are the same as men, or that they *want* to be the same as men. They want to be respected for their unique qualities. Men often say that women are too emotional, for example: women may well operate on a higher emotional level than men, but this is not necessarily bad, merely different. Women do not want men to attach a value of good or bad to a characteristic that might be said to be feminine. Respect implies a recognition of differences without condemnation.

Many women want to be free to pursue their own careers. In this area, too, they want respect. They want their husbands to recognize the talent and the income they bring into the marriage. They want their husbands to realize that they work as long a day as they do and that, therefore, housework should be shared.

Women want attention. All people require attention. This need not be a twenty-four-hour-a-day occupation; attention is day-to-day thoughtfulness. It is taking time to talk to one's spouse; it is complimenting the other person; it is recognizing the other person's needs and feelings.

Women want adoration—not all the time, but certainly when they are making love. They want to hear that they are beautiful, sexy, desirable. During lovemaking, a man and a woman must give each other undivided attention. This is what makes an affair so pleasurable for many women. When a sexual relationship is new and when two people are unknown to one another, they give each other attention. It could be so in marriage, too, but as we have seen, most of the women interviewed felt that sex with their husbands had become routine. Keeping eroticism in a marriage is work for both partners, but it is not impossible.

Women want friendship. They want someone who enjoys

doing at least some of the same activities they do. They want someone with whom they can talk and share their thoughts. They want a man who will listen and who will hold out a helping hand when necessary.

In short, women probably want what most men want.

Appendix

The interviews that appear in this book were taken from women who agreed to be interviewed. Some were taped, others were recorded in notes. The women were all asked to casually answer the following questions even though specific answers do not appear in all interviews.

1. What is your idea of love? Of sex? Of marriage?
2. Was something missing in your marriage that led you to seek an affair? Or did you do it just for the hell of it?
3. Had you ever thought about having an affair before you actually had one?
4. How did your first affair start?
5. How was your first affair different from your first sexual experience?
6. How did you meet the man?
7. How was the relationship different than the relationship between you and your husband?
8. How was extramarital sex different from the sex within your marriage?
9. Was there more than sex to the relationship?
10. How long did the first affair last, and how and why did it end?
11. Did the experience of the affair have lasting value?
12. Was the affair bad in any way?

13. How did the affair affect your relationship with your husband?
14. Did you fantasize about the other man when you were having sex with your husband?
15. Can you describe your most satisfying affair and explain why it was satisfying?
16. What were you looking for in an affair? Sex? A one-night stand? A friend?
17. How often have you had extramarital affairs?
18. Did you feel prepared for an affair?
19. How did you feel when you were having an affair?
20. Did you consider yourself to be in love with any of the men you had affairs with?
21. Are you still friends with any of the men you had affairs with?
22. What might you have done differently?
23. Did you find yourself experimenting sexually during the affair?
24. If you felt more free to experiment within the affair than you do within your marriage, can you explain why?
25. Have you ever read any sex manuals?
26. How much did a certain chemistry between you and the man you had an affair with affect you?
27. Were there any men you had the opportunity to have an affair with that you passed up? Do you regret having passed them up?
28. Have you had any lesbian affairs?
29. Were you afraid during any of the affairs? If so, of what?
30. Does your husband have affairs?
31. Do you have a mutual agreement with your husband regarding extramarital sex? If so, who suggested it?
32. What do you look for in a man when you want to have an affair?
33. What turns you on sexually?
34. Have your sexual preferences changed? Why?